105 SAP Basis (System Administration) Interview Questions with Answers & Explanations

By

N Thind & Kristine K

Copyright Notice

A Quick Interview; Check out how you fare!

Q1. How do you check if your system is a Unicode system?

We are planning to transport Objects between two SAP systems, one of which is Unicode and the other without Unicode.

Is it possible to do this? What are some of the issues I may face?

Answer;

There are a few ways to check if your system is Unicode.

On the SAP system

When logged on to the SAP system, click System -> Status

At OS level

Logon to OS level with SIDADM userid and run disp+work.

In the output, you will see if the system is Unicode.

To answer the second part of the questions; While it is possible to transport objects between a Unicode and a non Unicode SAP system, the process has to be approached with caution.

A general prerequisite for this type of transport is that the **R3trans** belonging to the system is used during both the import and export processes.

There are generally two classes of problems:

Technical transport problems (that is, the transport fails) and

Logical transport problems (the transport works, but the transported data does not fit in the target system).

a) Technical transport problems

o **'Exotic' languages**

Exotic languages are those for which a character is used within SAP that does not appear in the Latin 1 character set. An example is Azerbaijani (AZ), which is represented internally with the character 0xB89A.

Entries of language-dependent tables in such languages cannot be imported into ASCII systems. To ensure this, an R3trans version should always be used to import Unicode exports into ASCII systems.

o **Report texts in Japanese or Chinese**

Japanese and Chinese texts are displayed in ASCII with double-byte code pages. Depending on the available size of the target fields, the system may truncate texts during the conversion from Unicode to ASCII.

o **"Exotic" characters in table keys.**

Here, "duplicate key" errors may occur during the import.

o **Warnings with non-printable characters.**

During an ASCII import, some characters cannot be mapped to meaningful ASCII characters. When this is the case, the log displays corresponding messages and these messages may also contain non-printable characters.

b) Logical transport problems

o **Language-dependent character conversion**

Texts that contain non-Latin1 characters require a special character conversion. This happens automatically for language-dependent data if the R3trans transport program can recognize the language dependency (for example, for tables with a language field in the key).

o   **Special characters during the transport of Unicode to ASCII.**

In general, you cannot retain special characters when transporting from Unicode to ASCII if the target code page does not contain a corresponding character. These characters are mapped to '#', and in this case, a warning is issued in the import log.

o   **Transport of Customizing objects with address data**

Problems may occur during the transport from a non-Unicode system to a Unicode system, between two Unicode systems, and during the transport from a Unicode system to a non-Unicode system.

o   **Transport of screens from Unicode systems**

Transporting screens in the 3.1 or 4.0 format from Unicode systems may result in defective screen source codes, depending on the operating system used.

o   **Transport of texts (R3TR TEXT) and forms (R3TR FORM)**

These objects may be unreadable after a transport.

2. Transports from non-Unicode systems to Unicode systems

a) Technical transport problems

o   Up to now, there are no known technical transport problems.

b) Logical transport problems

o   **Language-dependent character conversion**

Texts that contain non-Latin1 characters require a special character conversion. This happens automatically for language-dependent data if the R3trans transport program can recognize the language dependency (for example, for tables with a language field in the key).

o   **Transport of Customizing objects with address data**

Problems may occur during the transport from a non-Unicode system to a Unicode system, between two Unicode systems, and during the transport from a Unicode system to a non-Unicode system.

Q2. In addition to outputting SAPscript forms or Smart Forms to a printer, we also need to send them as a PDF attachment to an email.
How can we do this?

Answer;

For SAPscript forms, from within your application print program, you need to call the SAPscript function module OPEN_FORM with the parameter DEVICE = 'MAIL''.

To send a Smart Form as an email PDF attachment, when calling the function module of the Smart Form from your application print program, you need to set CONTROL_PARAMETERS-DEVICE = 'MAIL' and the corresponding mail parameters.

In this way the OTF data is transferred to the SAPCONNECT interface and the PDF conversion is done there.

The device type used in the PDF conversion process is defined for each language in transaction SCOT as follows:
SCOT -> Settings -> 'Device type for Format Conversion'

Q3. We have tried to setup Single Sign-On with SAP logon tickets in Application Server ABAP and an error is displayed in the trace of transaction SM50. What kind of errors might you see and how would you fix them?

Answer;

While setting up Single Sign-On, you may see some of the following errors;

1. Invalid certificate

This error means that the signature of the SAP logon ticket cannot be checked. The reason for this error is often because

o   the certificate that is used is no longer valid.

o   the certificate that is used is not yet valid.

In the system that issues the ticket, check the validity of the certificate that is used. If necessary, create a new certificate which conforms to the above criteria.

2. An entry is missing from the access control list (ACS)

The ACL is client specific and must be maintained in the client in which you intend to use the SAP logon ticket. In the accepting system, use transaction STRUSTSSO2 to check whether the ACL is maintained in the corresponding client.

3. There is an obsolete entry in the ACL

When an entry is added to the ACL, the serial number of the certificate is also added. If you have created a new certificate in the system that issues the ticket and its serial number is different from the serial number used previously, you must update the entry in the ACL also.

4. The certificate does not exist in the certificate list

This error means that the certificate of the issuing system cannot be found. The reason for this error is often because

o   the certificate of the issuing system is not in the certificate list of the system Personal Security Environment (PSE) in the accepting system.

o   there is an obsolete certificate of the issuing system in the certificate list of the accepting system (for example, after the regeneration of a key pair in the issuing system).

o   the accepting system is configured so that a different PSE is used to verify the logon ticket which the certificate of the accepting system does not contain.

5. Receiver data is incorrect

For the SAP assertion ticket, the receiver data must match the current system data. Therefore, you must check the entries in the issuing system.

6. No digital signature could be generated

To issue a digital signature, the system requires a PSE. The PSE is stored on the file system of the application server and additional meta information about the file is saved in the database. If you now change the file directly at file system level, inconsistencies may occur. In particular, when the system issues an SAP logon ticket that is digitally signed by the application server, the trace displays the following additional entry:

N *** ERROR => Ticket creation failed with rc = 1441801. [ssoxxkrn.c 704

To correct this problem, proceed as follows:
 - Call transaction STRUST
 - Double-click the entry "System PSE"
 - From the menu, select "PSE > Save as.. ."
 - Select the option "System PSE"
 - Confirm the dialogs that follow
         => As a result, the PSE is saved again in the file system and the database tables are cleaned up.

Q4. When would you recommend that a company uses Virtual Host Names instead of physical host names when installing an SAP system. How would you do this installation?

Answer;

Using virtual host names might be useful when you want to quickly move SAP servers or complete server landscapes to other new hardware without having to perform a reinstallation or complicated reconfiguration.

Another reason might be the naming convention for DNS names specified in the security policy of your company – if, for example, an application must run with a unique virtual host name.

Before you install your SAP system using a virtual host name, you must first prepare your operating system and check whether it is configured properly for using virtual host names.

1. Define a new DNS A-record for each virtual host name.
Example for a DNS A-record: 10.67.4.28 enterprise
I do not recommend using DNS CNAMES.

2. Make sure that the reverse DNS lookup for this new name works properly.

3. Add the IP address to the network card configuration.

4. Check whether the IP address was successfully bound by opening a command prompt and entering the ipconfig command.

5. Check whether the reverse DNS lookup works correctly with the nslookup

command (for example, nslookup <ip-of-enterprise>).

6.   Check whether the local IPv4 address is returned with the ping command (for example, ping –a enterprise).

7.   Check whether the reverse DNS lookup works correctly with the nslookup command (for example, nslookup <ip-of-enterprise>).

8.   To use the virtual hostname enterprise, configure the Windows operating system as follows:

a.   Add the value DisableStrictNameChecking to the registry:
HKEY_LOCAL_MACHINE\SYSTEM\CurrentControlSet\Services\lanmanserver\parameter s

b.   Add a value DisableStrictNameChecking of type DWORD set to 1.

c.   To apply the changes, either reboot your system or restart the Windows Server service without rebooting.

d.   Add the value BackConnectionHostnames:
HKEY_LOCAL_MACHINE\SYSTEM\CurrentControlSet\Control\Lsa\MSV1_0

e.   Add the new multi-string value BackConnectionHostNames.
Enter the fully qualified domain name (FQDN) (in our example: enterprise.wdf.sap.corp) and the short name.

To use virtual host names, you do not have to change the local hosts file: %windir% \system32\drivers\etc\hosts.

However, you can use a virtual host name that only works locally to allow the operating system to "find itself" using a virtual name.

Then add the name to the local hosts file.

9.   Check whether the virtual host names work properly in Windows.

If they do not work properly, you get an Access denied error. In this case, correct the registry keys and values.

Use the following options to perform the checks:

o   Enter the command: net view \\virtualhostname

If you get the message Access denied, either the registry keys are not correctly set, or you have to reboot your Windows operating system.

o   Use the net view \\virtualhostname command from other servers.

If you get the error A duplicate name exists on the network, the key DisableStrictNameChecking is not correctly set.

o   Use the SAP MMC and connect to computer virtualhostname:

Open the SAP MMC.

Select File –> Add/remove Snap-in ...

Select Computer Management and choose Add.

Click OK.

To install your system using a Virtual Host Name, you must;

1.   Start SAPinst from a command prompt and execute the following case-sensitive command:

SAPINST_USE_HOSTNAME=<virtualname>

2.   Proceed as described in the installation guide.

After the installation has finished successfully, your system is available in the SAP MMC.

The system uses the virtual host name.

In our example, the host name is PWDF1000 and the virtual host name is ENTERPRISE.

Q5. Our production Database size is less than 100 GB and daily backups are possible.

Can you advice what our database backup strategy should look like and how should faulty backups be treated?

Answer;

SAP data is stored in a relational database. A data backup consists of database files and SAP files such as programs, log files, and so on, which are stored centrally under /usr/sap/... .

You use operating system tools to back up this directory tree, which is part of the hierarchical file system. As this data generally only changes when profile parameters are modified or after an upgrade, you only need to perform a backup in such cases.

Since it is generally very dynamic, SAP data requires a comprehensive security strategy.

The size of the database is less than 100 GB and daily backups are possible.

If the SAP System does not have to be available after 18:00, you can perform the backup offline.

Alternatively, you can perform the backup at a time when the transaction load is low. A full backup of the data (without log redo information) fits onto two tapes, if DLT techniques are used.

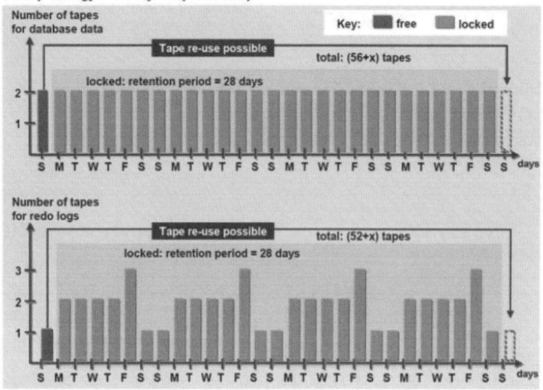

Backup Strategy with Daily Complete Backups

To be able to deal with a faulty backup, several generations of backups have to be available.

Therefore, for this example, the retention period is set to 28 days and consequently 27 backup generations are available in the event of database failure.

The tape pool ought to contain several reserve tapes, shown as "+ x" in the above graphic. The additional tapes – I recommend approximately 30% of the required number – are intended as a reserve in case the amount of data to be backed up greatly increases or an extra unplanned backup becomes necessary.

Using a separate tape pool, you also need to back up the redo log information generated during the day, which is temporarily stored on a separate large disk until the tape backup.

As this data is necessary to recover a database after restoring a data backup, never set the retention period for the redo log tapes to less than the retention period for the data backup tapes. Particularly in the case of an online backup, it is best to always back up redo logs directly after the data backup.

Without redo log information the online backup is worthless.

As the redo log information is much more dynamic than the database data, even more reserve tapes are required.

I recommend you to back up the redo logs twice for extra security, so that you need 2 x (52 + x) tapes in the redo log tape pool.

Contents

1 We plan to install SAP ECC system with SQL Database and we would like to use the new compression functionality of SQL while installing our production server, how we should go with this process?

SAP uses the executable r3load for creating new tables during the installation, migration and upgrade. R3load does not take care of SAP profile parameters. Since there is no way to keep the compression type of the SAP Data Dictionary synchronized with the compression type of r3load, the compression type of new (and even existing) tables might change during an SAP upgrade. Therefore, re-compress these tables using report MSSCOMPRESS after an SAP upgrade.

We can change the default compression type of r3load by modifying the file DDLMSS.TPL, which is located in the SAPINST directory and on the exports DVDs. The template file DLMSS.TPL starts with the following lines:

```
prikey: BEFORE_LOAD ORDER_BY_PKEY
seckey: AFTER_LOAD
cretab: CREATE TABLE &tab_name&
( /{ &fld_name& &fld_desc& /-, /} )
# to deactivate row compression on SQL 2008 and higher
# add &norowcompression& after the closing bracket:
# cretab: CREATE TABLE &tab_name&
# ( /{ &fld_name& &fld_desc& /-, /} ) &norowcompression&
```

We have following option for SQL database compression

- *&norowcompression&: r3load does not use any compression type*
- *&compression_none&: r3load uses compression type NONE*
- *&compression_row&: r3load uses compression type ROW*
- *&compression_page&: r3load uses compression type PAGE*

The template file DDLMSS.TPL is created using the executable r3ldctl.exe. The newest version of r3ldctl creates a template with page compression for tables and indexes.

2   **In our solution Manager System there are lot of inconsistencies in the entries in SLD and SMSY, before upgrading out Solution Manager System we would like to remove these in consistent entries from our Solution Manager System, what are the possibilities?**

Generally systems created manually in the Solution Manager System maintenance before the landscape fetch from SLD has been enabled may cause duplicate entries for the manually created ones.

In case of ABAP and Java systems such conflicts can be resolved by using a wizard **"Manage Conflicts for Technical Systems".**

Systems manually created after the fetch from SLD will not be considered as duplicates in the wizard.

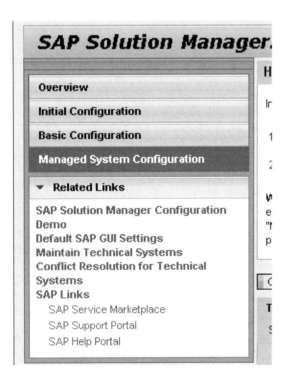

Select "Conflict Resolution for Technical Systems" from the "Related Links" of the "Managed System Configuration".

Potential

3　　We have a significant usage of our JAVA stack for our Netweaver system, mainly http applications we have developed for our organisation, users generally complains about system performance of the JAVA stack, how we can live up to their expectations in terms of response time? What measures we can take to ensure proper tuning and enhancement in the response time?

There are two major areas to work on performance part of the java stack,

Tuning the Operating System

Most general tuning considerations for an operating system that will run Java and WAS must include:

- OS version and patch level of the OS, Vendors keep updating the bugs as an when they occurred.

- Network check in terms of response time between proxies, packages lost rate, and so on.

- TCP/IP connection handling at OS level to ensure that the OS can handle the desired number of connections.

- Memory buffers for disk I/O can be tuned to handle the amount of I/O, which is expected on the system. For example, for a WAS central instance with a database we recommend bigger I/O buffers and also several separate physical hard drives where the database files and log files are spread.
- Number of opened file descriptors, and so on.

Tuning JVM settings

SAP provides tuning recommendations per OS/JVM in several SAP Notes.
The recommendations are based on experience from SAP internal testing and already productive customer systems.

4   **For the ABAP Webdynpro applications we need to have Full Qualified Domain Name for our SAP-ABAP system while calling the application, how many ways we achieve this?**

A Fully Qualified Domain Name will be set via multiple ways some them are

Setting up the parameter in SAP Profile **SAPLOCALHOSTFULL**, ICM takes the FQDN value from this parameter while starting up the system.

Setting up ICM parameter **icm/host_name_full** will also result in setting up the FQDN

5   **In our Production operations, Import of one of the TR has been hanged due to some reason; we need to investigate the cause, what are the possible ways to find out the cause to this situation?**

First to investigate the issue we will have to involve several components of the SAP system,

- OS Space for /usr/sap/trans folder should be checked.
- Check for Free Background Process availability
- Check TP Log and system Log
- Check dev_evt for any errors
- Check Sm37 for any RDD* jobs failures
- Delete the transport from import monitor and restart the transport and see how it goes ... if required delete the entries from TRBAT and TRJOB tables and re-execute import.

These are some of the things which will help us resolve the error.

6   **We observed that after truncating / backup the size of the transaction log file remains same we could not get hold of the unused space for our SQL Database, Is there any way we can get back that space if yes how?**

Yes that's correct, the backup operation or the Truncate method does not reduce the log file size. To reduce the size of the transaction log file, you must shrink the transaction log file. To shrink a transaction log file to the requested size and to remove the unused pages, you must use the DBCC SHRINKFILE operation.

But one we thing we have to take into considerations while shrinking the Log file that the DBCC SHRINKFILE Transact-SQL statement can only shrink the inactive part inside the log file.

Shrinking the transaction log

DBCC SHRINKFILE

7   **Our users are printing a lot of data out of our SAP System, sometime we have printer outages also and we couldn't print ... So User again has to run the report and print, which in turns consuming lot of resources for this duplication running reports twice, Is there any other way we can reduce this load? Has there been any consideration from SAP to this problem? If yes how we should work with it.**

The Situation is likely to happen many times in real life to lot of customers, SAP has definitely thought and worked on this solution. SAP when selected a document for printing creates a Spool Request which stores partly formatted data.

While sending to print on actual device an Output Request is created with Spool request data and sent for printing to specific device. An Output request can have different attributes like target printer or no of copies.

So once we have a Spool request number we can print data any number of times on any defined printer in SAP system, so we do not have to run the report again just to print it.

By differentiating between Spool request and output request SAP provides a means for storing the data temporarily.

8   We are running our all SAP systems in Virtual Environment to get the benefits of virtual technology to add hardware resources to the system dynamically when the system are up and running, Several times we seen there is a deadlock occurring in our system due the these resources but we cannot change any configuration in SAP to get rid of this Deadlock on the go, Can we achieve any dynamic configuration in SAP system?

Starting from SAP Netweaver 7.1 we have dynamic control over the resources of SAP system.

Dynamic work processes enable the work process configuration of the SAP NetWeaver Application Server (AS ABAP) to be modified in accordance with the current specifications while the system is running. This includes restarting new work processes and closing work processes no longer needed.

There are two ways to achieve this

Reserved (restricted) work processes

These types of Work Process are reserved in the system and will be used in accordance with the situation. This type of work processes are always of Type Dialog only. The parameter to control these reserved work processes is rdisp/`wp_no_restricted`

Work processes started dynamically

If the dynamic work processes are active (**rdisp/dynamic_wp_check=TRUE**), the system can start new work processes up to the limit specified in **rdisp/wp_max_no** in order to resolve deadlocks. Dynamic work processes can have different types (dialog, batch, update, and so on).

9   **During a production usage of the system we have a Roll Out data conversion planned, what are the things from basis perspective should be take into account for a smooth day today operation and timely completion of Data Conversion step for our Roll-Out Project?**

During the data conversion stage of the roll out projects, we have to plan data conversion activity considering some basic aspects of SAP Administration.

- **No of Background Process**: We must Plan/add no of background process to the application server depending on the data load we will have. We can achieve this easily via adding a temporary application server to the server
- **No of Update Process**: Generally during Data Conversion there are lot of Updates to the DB, so Update work process also needs to adjusted
- **Lock Table Entries**: Lot of Updates means lot of Locks needs on the DB. So the lock entry tables should be big enough to hold the lock entries.
- **Work Flows**: We can think of switching off unwanted Workflows during the activity.
- **Physical memory**: If needed add more Physical memory to server or add more temporary application servers
- **Buffer tuning** : extend buffers adequately for the activity
- **Database Tuning**: if required tune up the database beforehand, update optimizer statistics to cater huge data changes.

There are some of the points we should be taking into consideration before starting the data conversion activity on Production server.

10   **We frequently encounter OutOfMemory error in our Java stack, what might be the possible causes and explain a bit about them in detail.**

The OutOfMemory dump in Java occurs when application is trying load itself in the memory but there is no memory left for the application to load.

There is a possibility of Low Heap Memory allocated to Java Instance.

There is a possibility of application requesting too much memory due to programming deficiency.

In Java all the memory areas are called generations Young Generation, Tenured Generation & Permanent Generation.

The active objects are always placed in Young Generation first and once they no longer active they will be moved to tenured generation for future use. Permanent Generation hold the entire permanent object in Java (Methods, Class, etc.) and they are static in nature.

Objects moved through these areas and finally deleted via a process called Garbage Collection. In Java we have two types of Garbage Collections such as Minor Garbage Collection and Full Garbage Collection.

The objects marked for deletion will be wiped out during the process.

11   **What are the parameters which control the Heap Memory in Java, and what are the recommended values to get better performance for your Java Applications.**

- **-Xms** initial size of the heap space.
- **-Xmx** maximum size of the heap space.
- **-XX:NewSize** initial size of the young generation Memory.
- **-XX:MaxNewSize** maximum size of the young generation Memory.

SAP generally recommends putting values for –Xms = -Xmx same to Max Heap Space to avoid below problems:

Java Start-up Time: If the initial size is not enough then resizing has to occur in the memory which can lead to a bad stat times for Java Stack.

Application Performance: If resizing happens a lot in the memory due to insufficient memory lot of objects have to be moved around resulting in poor performance

12 How will you register SAP ABAP systems in existing SLD?

To register the SAP ABAP system in existing SLD please proceeds as follow:

Logon to SAP ABAP instance
T Code RZ70

Enter the required details of SLD host and Gateway Service of you SLD

Activate your changes and schedule the job for updating SLD contents periodically.

13 How we will manage all SAP ABAP only systems in JAVA only SLD?

To register ABAP only system in SLD we need a Gateway service to communicate to the SLD server. A JAVA only system has no gateway installed by default at the time of installation.

Just add following lined in your SCS instance Start up profile will start a Standalone Gateway on your server; please adapt the SID, SCS, and hostname with the values.

Restart the J2EE and you have a gateway running.

  #----

    Start SAP gateway service

#----

GW = $(DIREXECUTABLE)/gwrd$(FT_EXE)

Start_Program_02 = local $(_GW) pf=$(DIR_PROFILE)/<SID>_SCSXX_<hostname>

Then provide all the details in RZ70 to send data to your SLD server.

14   Can you describe some common ABAP Dumps with possible solution?

Some common ABAP dumps and possible solution are as below:

SYSTEM_CORE_DUMPED

In most situations SYSTEM_CORE_DUMPED is related to the R/3 system kernel. As generally advised and in keeping with best practice upgrade to the latest available kernel patch to solve the issue

We need detailed analysis of the core dump at the Kernel will provide more reasons behind the dump.

TSV_TNEW_PAGE_ALLOC_FAILED

DUMP 'TSV_TNEW_PAGE_ALLOC_FAILED' simply indicates exhausted available SAP memory resources by a process.

When this DUMP is reported more memory was requested by the SAP system because the program needed to expand an internal table. The memory resource was not available. When the available Extended Memory is exhausted the process will enter PRIV mode (seen in SM50) and will start to use Heap Memory (local memory).

SYSTEM_NO_TASK_STORAGE

SYSTEM_NO_TASK_STORAGE dumps are also address space/memory related.

This dump in general relates to 32-bit address space limitation regarding memory resources. On 32-bit platforms the long term solution is to use 64bit.

Another possible cause for the dump SYSTEM_NO_TASK_STORAGE is running an old SAP collector. SAP does recommend running with the latest available collector.

CALL_FUNCTION_SINGLE_LOGIN_REJ

This dump is generally reported when there is insufficient authorization to login to the trusted system. 4 different error codes are related to CALL_FUNCTION_SINGLE_LOGIN_REJ

0 - Incorrect logon data for valid security ID.

1 - Calling system is not a Trusted System or security ID is invalid.

2 - Either user does not have RFC authorization (authorization object S_RFCACL), or a logon was performed using one of the protected users DDIC or SAP*.

3 - Time stamp of the logon data is invalid.

PXA_NO_SHARED_MEMORY

DUMP PXA_NO_SHARED_MEMORY occurs there is not enough contiguous address space to create the buffer of size X MB Approx. (where x is size in megabytes).

May be relevant as some DLLs may be positioned that are stopping the creation of this large buffer on Windows platforms.

15   We have been hitting ORA-08102: index key not found several times during our production operations what might be the possible solution?

The error clearly shows that index key was not found for an object in the table. Index for the tables mentioned in the error (ACCTHD) in the above case was corrupted. Hence DB action DEL (delete) is failing on these tables. I have checked several forums with the error code ORA-8102 and in most of them suggested rebuilding the index for all tables.

Run the below query on the set of tables to get list if index to be rebuild for the given table

select index_name, owner from dba_indexes where table_name='<table_name_uppercase>';

From the list of Index displayed from the above query run the below command to generate the index and wait till you receive the confirmation "Index altered."

16   We are planning our landscape globally and we need to develop the strategy for creating our central SLD, we have been advised to have more than one SLD in landscape what are the possible reasons behind this recommendation?

For a global landscape SAP have several strategies towards SLD, it always advised to have more than one SLD in such a big landscape, and moreover many applications rely on SLD data. Among these are most prominently - SAP NetWeaver Process Integration (PI), WebDynpro for Java, and the SAP Solution Manager, some of the options we have are as follows:

- **Areas in front of and behind a firewall**: If something needs to be available in front of and behind a firewall, you need at least two systems.

- **Separation of development, quality assurance, and productive systems**: Most easily and most importantly this can be explained for PI - Business Systems are developed before they are meant to be used productively. The easiest way to separate non-productive and productive state is to separate the development and productive SLD.

- **Separation of managing and managed systems:** The SAP Solution Manager does not recommend to have runtime dependencies to productive systems but on the other hand recommends to have a "local" SLD activated on the SAP Solution Manager system: Since SLD data are crucial for all applications mentioned earlier, at least one more SLD is required if any other SLD client application is used

- **Having 24/7 business hours does not allow for maintenance causing downtime**: A backup SLD system is needed to ensure the availability of SLD data.

Having extremely high security requirements, where certain SLD systems need to be isolated from the net may also require isolated SLD systems.

17 What is the significance of ASU Toolbox in upgrade and Unicode conversion process of ECC system? And how it can be significantly used with Upgrade accelerator

The so called Application-Specific Upgrade (ASU) toolbox is one of the tools which customers can use during the upgrade implementation.

The ASU toolbox

- provides you a detailed task overview of steps which you have to perform before and after your technical upgrade

- shows you a description of each step, links to the related SAP notes, and gives you the possibility to insert comments regarding this step
- gives you the chance to plan and organize your pre and post upgrade tasks to your own needs
- enables you to transport the once generated task list within your whole upgrade landscape
- and helps you to get the system quickly and with a minimum of effort and cost into a stable condition

The Upgrade Accelerator is a tool which is included in the upgrade procedure itself and can also be used to support customers during the upgrade implementation.

The Upgrade Accelerator

- helps you to get the system in a stable condition
- performs the manual application-specific pre-upgrade steps automatically during the PREPARE and the POST downtime phases
- is called via SAPup during the prepare phase RUN_UACC_PREP and the post downtime phase RUN_UACC_POST
- decreases the number and effort of manually triggered application-specific pre-upgrade steps

18 What are the available options we have to for Temse Storage system in any SAP System?

The SAP spool system uses the Temse storage system to store output data. The TemSe database is also used for storing background processing job logs and other sequential objects that are temporary in nature.

Temse database storage requirements are generally depends on the system and the printing usage of the system. We have two options to save these data either in SAP's own Database or at the operating system.
These two options are controlled with the help of below parameter.

rspo/store_location = G or db

Value **G** indicates storage at OS level, and **db** indicates storage location at DB.

19   **What are the pros and cons towards deciding the storage location of TemSe Database? We are expecting a huge amount of printing usage.**

Storage Method - File system

The File system storage for TemSe is quite fast and better performance.

The disadvantage with this storage method would be, always need to backup and restore with operating systems tool separately from database. In case of hard restore there might be chances of inconsistencies between files and Temse Mgmt. database of SAP.

Storage Method - Database

Unlike file system storage, with database method TemSe database will be backed up with a DB tools and no need to have separate database backups. Consistency in case of DB restored is ensured.

Disadvantage would be slower in performance than file system storage and increase DB load.

20   **The Dialog Multiplexing concept of SAP, how does this works and helps in real implementations?**

Work Process multiplexing means that a system functions whose contents are logically connected but consists of multiple sub-steps can be processed by various dialog steps.

The successive dialog steps for the same user can be processed in different work processes.

Due to this multiplexing several users can use one dialog process and we don't need more work process to cater user requests in real life.

21   **We are planning a SAP BW implementation for our 7 Sites across the world, we are expecting a huge amount of data stored in our BW system, and we would like to explore the options for designing our BW database.**

For very large implementation of SAP BW, for the database considerations there are few considerations towards designing the databases.

Some of the designers recommend using partitioned table and indexes. Partitioned tables allow data to be split into smaller, easily manageable units called partitions. Partitions can store data in different data segments and we can manage them individually.

Due to heavy usage of SAP BW systems for reporting purposes, with partitioned tables all the operations can be performed in parallel on the same table or index.

22   **Difference between Dictionary managed tablespace (DMT) and Locally managed tablespace (LMT)**

Locally Managed Tablespaces:

A tablespace that manages its own extents maintains a bitmap in each datafile to keep track of the free or used status of blocks in that datafile. Each bit in the bitmap corresponds to a group of blocks. When an extent is allocated or freed for reuse, Oracle changes the bitmap values to show the new status of the blocks. These changes do not generate rollback information because they do not update tables (like sys.uet$, sys.fet$) in the data dictionary (except for special cases such as tablespace quota information).

When you create a locally managed tablespace, header bitmaps are created for each datafile. If more datafiles are added, new header bitmaps are created for each added file.

Local management of extents automatically tracks adjacent free space, eliminating the need to coalesce free extents. The sizes of extents that are managed locally can be determined automatically by the system. Alternatively, all extents can have the same size in a locally managed tablespace.

Dictionary Managed Tablespaces:

In DMT, to keep track of the free or used status of blocks, oracle uses data dictionary tables. When an extent is allocated or freed for reuse, free space is recorded in the SYS.FET$ table, and used space in the SYS.UET$ table. Whenever space is required in one of these tablespaces, the ST (space transaction) enqueue latch must be obtained to do insert and deletes against these tables. As only one process can acquire the ST enque at a given time, this often lead to contention. These changes generate rollback information because they update tables (like sys.uet$, sys.fet$) in the data dictionary.

Advantages of Locally Managed Tablespaces (LMT) over Dictionary Managed Tablespaces (DMT):

1. Reduced recursive space management
2. Reduced contention on data dictionary tables
3. No rollback generated
4. No coalescing required

23 **We have a quite old SAP R3 system with managed tablespaces and recently we have been reviewing benefits of Locally managed tablespaces and we would like to convert the tablespaces, we need to perform reorganisation of DB, can we discuss this way forward?**

The Reorganization activity generally initiated due to tablespace conversions as per requirement here or to gain the space from the fragmented tables.

One more reason also might be due to relocate certain tables between the disks or tablespaces.

The general procedure for reorganization would be:

- Export tables
- Drop exported tables
- Recreate Tablespaces in required
- Import the tables again

We have online method of reorganizations of the tables as well.

24   We need to perform Segment Shrinking with Oracle 10G, what are the advantages and procedure for this activity?

Segment Shrinking is considered a viable alternative towards table reorganization. It defragments a segment and gain more free space. Generally segment shrinking performs combining used segments.

We cannot move tables between tablespaces with segment shrinking; it actually works within the tablespace.

With BRtools release 700 we can perform segment shrinking with BRSPACE.

25   During a SAP system start-up what are the profiles used and how they read in sequence? Can you describe then in a bit detail?

The sequence of the profiles used during the start process of SAP system as below

1. Startup Profile

Startup profile defines which database to start for central and dialog instances. On ABAP system IGS Watchdog, ABAP dispatcher and message server is started with the help of Startup Profile.

2. Default Profile

Default Profile is common to all the instances and it is ready by all instance while start up. It contains system wide settings such as DB Name, Enque Server name etc.

3. Instance Profile

Instance profiles are specific for instance and parameters will be applied to only specific instance. It contains memory parameters, no of process etc. for the particular instance.

26   **What are the installation options are available for SAP customers? Can you describe some of the examples with solutions?**

There are 3 different installation options are available to choose from as below:

ABAP Only

In this installation option there will be only ABAP stack installed, and customers can only use functionalities related to ABAP. Solutions like SAP ECC, SAP SRM

ABAP + Java

In this installation option there will be both stacks ABAP and well as JAVA available for customers to use. Solutions like SAP PI, SAP ECC

JAVA Only

In this installation option only JAVA stack will be installed and available for use. Solutions like SAP EP, SAP CE.

27   **Currently in our ECC landscape we have a SAP Netweaver 7.0 EHP2 system installed which we use for our Enterprise Portal and we are planning to use SAP MDM in our Landscape, can we use our Enterprise portal for MDM? If yes how we can proceed?**

Yes we can use the same SAP Netweaver 7.0 EHP2 system for your SAP MDM 7.1. What we need to do is install an additional Usage type MDM on the same Netweaver server as below:

1. Check the additional usage type guide for installation and compatibility with your existing system
2. Download required media from service market place
3. Place media in your EPS\in dir for the server
4. Start JSPM and select install additional usage type
5. Check the version and component after your inbox scan
6. Deploy the component with JSPM
7. Apply patch if any required for your additional component

Result

You are now having an additional usage type installed on the server.

28 Can you describe the Add-on Installation Process in Detail?

SAP has provided a comprehensive tool to install and update all your SAP systems Add-on Packages, now even enhancement packages can also be installed with SAINT.

There are few simple steps to install/update an Add-on in SAP system.

1. Define the installation queue.

With SAINT we can install multiple add-ons at the same time, so download all the required files and put in your inbox and SAINT will calculate and define the queue in correct sequence for installation.

With solution manager you can create a stack definition file as well for upload to SAINT.

2. Optional: Include modification adjustment transports into the installation queue.

This step allows you to specify the transport request you create for modification with the Add-On's may be in your development/Sandbox system.

3. Define the start options or check those selected.

You can define start options for the individual modules according to your system requirements. If you confirm the dialog field without changing any settings, the import tool assumes the default start options, according to the selected import mode. If you change any settings, you can save them as a template for future import activities.

4. Install the queue.

The selected start options determine when the queue installation will begin. If you have, for example, selected the Immediate Start option for the Preparation module then the installation starts immediately after confirming the start options.

Depending on the import mode selected the Add-On Installation Tool executes the installation.

29   **Please describe the procedure to implement patch using JSPM for SAP Netweaver Java system.**

We patch all the java components of an SAP system with a tool called JSPM (Java Support Package Manager); the procedure to update the software components is as below:

Prerequisites

- The AS Java and the database have been backed up.
- The support packages you want to apply have been downloaded to the global EPS inbox directory /usr/sap/trans/EPS/in.
- The <SID>adm user has Read permissions for the global EPS inbox directory usr/sap/trans/EPS/in.
- There is enough disk space.

Procedure

- Choose the Deployment tab.
- Select the Package Type (Single Support Packages)
- All the available software components from your system which can be patched will be shown.

Specify the Queue

You can specify which software components you want to update and to which patch level and define the queue. JSPM automatically check all the required files from inbox and show the status of the files which can be deployed.

Deploy Queue

JSPM starts the deployment of the software components that you selected. The status of all software components changes to SCHEDULED.

If you have selected to update the kernel, and if your system is distributed, during the deployment you are first prompted to stop the primary application server instance and any running dialog instances, and to choose Next.
Then you are prompted to start the primary application server instance and to choose Next.

Completed

Check the logs for any errors.

30   **We are experiencing a huge load on some of our servers, even though there are more servers which are less utilized by the end users. We have to streamline this server usage so that all servers should be used for better performance, how we can achieve this?**

These situations are likely to occur if we don't use SAP Logon Load Balancing feature provided by SAP. With Logon Load Balancing we can distribute all end users to available application servers. We can create logon groups as below:

1. We can create Logon groups with T code SMLG

2. In the Create/Change Entry dialog box, you can configure the following options:

   o   Group assignment: The Name of the logon Group
   o   Instance (application server): select the application server to be added to this group, for adding multiple application servers we have to perform above step repeatedly.

- Response time: Specify the Response time for the application servers for this logon groups and system automatically sets a homogeneous value for all groups that are associated with that instance.
- Users: The maximum number of configured users who can be logged on to an instance.

Save entries and your Logon group is ready to be used.

31   In our BW system with multiple hosts or instances for loading processes: Regardless of the number of source systems how we should configure Load Balancing

To configure load balancing in above scenario please follow the steps below:

- Create a logon group in the BW system, then assign instances to it and activate dynamic RFC load balancing. To do this, choose Tools CCMS Configuration Logon Groups (transaction SMLG).

- If a suitable logon group already exists, you can adapt this logon group using the steps listed below.

- To create a logon group, call the CCMS: Logon Group Maintenance screen and press the Create Assignment (Create Assignment) button.

- In the dialog box that appears, choose the Assignment tab and enter a name for the logon group.

- Specify the instance that you want to add to the logon group.

- Activate dynamic RFC load balancing for the logon group. To do this, choose the Assignment tab and the Group Specific group frame and select the Allow External RFC field.

- Press the Apply (Apply) button.

- To add more instances to the logon group, call the CCMS: Logon Group Maintenance screen and press the Create Assignment (Create Assignment) button again.

- In the dialog box that appears, select the logon group you created before and specify the next instance that you want to add to the logon group.

- Press the Apply (Apply) button.

- Repeat steps 7 to 9 for all instances that you want to add to the logon group.

- Save your settings on the CCSM: Logon Group Maintenance screen.

- In the logon group maintenance transaction, the system now displays every instance that you have assigned to the logon group.

32   What are the options available for setting up Load Balancing for Background process in BW system for a better utilization of our application servers?

For setting up the parallel processing for background process you can choose one of the following options for load balancing:

- Server: You can select a certain application server for background processing.

- Host: If you select a host, job processing is balanced on the host server. The overview of the SAP application servers (transaction SM51) shows which application servers are running on the host.

- Server Group: If you select a server group, job processing is balanced on the servers in the group.

You can create server groups for background processing using transaction SM61.

33 How to set Parallel Processing of BW Processes in SAP BW system?

We can follow the below procedure to setup parallel processing:

- In the Data Warehousing Workbench choose Administration ->Current Settings -> Batch Manager or transaction RSBATCH.

- The screen BW Background Management, Logs and Tools appears.

- On the tab page Background and Parallel Processes in the group frame Settings for Parallel Processing, select a process type by choosing Select Process.

- Choose Parameter Settings.

- The Settings for Parallel Processing dialog box appears.

- Under Number of Processes, define the maximum number of work processes that should be used to process the BW process.

- If you enter 1, the BW process is processed serially.

- If you enter a number greater than 1, the BW process is processed in parallel.

- In the Parallel Processing group frame, make the relevant settings for parallel processing in the background:

  - Enter a job class for defining the job priority.

- The job priority defines how the jobs are distributed among the available background work processes.

- In the group frame Parallel Processing, you can define whether parallel processing should take place in dialog work processes or in background work processes for the processes ODSACTIVAT, ODSSID and ODSREQUDEL for the DataStore object.

- If you select Dialog, you can define the load distribution of an RFC server group as Server Group for Parallel Dialog Processing.

- You can create RFC server groups in transaction RZ12. More information: Defining RFC Groups for Parallel Processing Jobs

- To write the settings to a transport request, choose This graphic is explained in the accompanying text Transport. The entries in tables RSBATCHPARALLEL and RSBATCHSERVER (for hosts and server groups) are written on a transport request of the Change and Transport System.

- Save your entries.
- Set parallel processing for a specific BW process in the (variant) maintenance of the process

34 **We are planning to have a JAVA only system as our SLD and we learned that we need a standalone gateway to push our ABAP SLD data how we can install Standalone Gateway?**

To install a standalone gateway for Windows NT you need to access the installation program "r3gwinst.exe". You will find this program on the "Presentation CD". The program is also available in the subdirectory \NT\i386\ as from Release 3.0D (same procedure under UNIX).

This directory contains all of the necessary files for installing an R/3 standalone gateway.

Select the SAP system name <SID>

The actual installation can only be carried out by a user with administrator authorization on the SAP Internet Gateway server.

Start the program "r3gwinst.exe" and answer the installation questions.

This will complete the installation of Standalone Gateway.

We can install standalone gateway through sapinst as well.

35 **Describe some of the sap gateway security parameters?**

There are several parameters used during setting up the security measures on the SAP Gateway, some of them are as below:

35.1.1.1.1 gw/acl_file

This parameter specifies the name of an ACL file. With an ACL (access control list) you can configure who is permitted to connect to the gateway.

- The same ACL file is used for the standard port and for the SNC port of the gateway.

- If the specified ACL file does not exist or is erroneous, the gateway immediately closes.

If the parameter is not set, access control is not valid.

35.1.1.1.2 gw/acl_mode

This parameter defines the behaviour of the gateway, if an ACL file (gw/sec_info or gw/reg_info) does not exist.

The following values are permitted:

- 0: There is no restriction with starting external servers or registering servers.
- 1: External and registered servers are only permitted within the system (application servers of the same system). All other servers are rejected or have to be maintained in the respective files.

35.1.1.1.3 gw/sec_info

File with the security information.

Any unauthorized starting of external programs can be prevented by maintaining the file secinfo in the data directory of the gateway instance.

35.1.1.1.4 gw/tcp_security

These parameters can be used to protect external programs against being started.

If this parameter has the value 1, the information in file gw/sec_info is read. The gateway establishes from the entries in this file whether the user has the authority to start external programs.

35.1.1.1.5 gw/reg_info

File with the security information for registered programs.

Unauthorized registration of programs can be prevented by maintaining the file reginfo in the data directory of the gateway instance.

If the file exists, the system searches for valid registration entries in this list. If there are none, the system searches, as up to now too, in the gw/sec_info file.

36   **Can you describe some of the standard basis report we have in SAP system regardless of the version used?**

There are several programs in SAP we can use regardless of the SAP Version some of them are:

- RSCOLL00   Performance Collector
- RSBPCOLL   Collect Values for statistics
- RSSNAPDL   Delete ABAP Dumps
- RSTRFCER   Delete EXEC LUWs
- RSBPSTDE   Delete old job statistics
- RSBTCPRIDEL   Reorganization of Print Parameters for Background Jobs
- RSPO1041   Delete old Spool Files
- RSPO1043   Spool Data-Consistency check in Background (SP12)
- RSBDCREO   Delete Old Batch input Files
- SAPconnect: Start Send Process Fax/Email
- RSTBPDEL   Delete Entries in DBTABLOG
- RSARFCER   Deletes entries in arfcstate and arfcdata for RFCs (ARFC)
- RSTRFCES   Deletes tRFC and qRFC entries (arfcrstate, trfcqout)
- RSTS0024   Deletes job log headers from TST01 that are older than jobs in TBTCO
- SBAL_DELETE   deletes application logs (BALHDR)
- RBDCPCLR   Deletes Obsolete change pointers
- RSARFCEX   Retries entries in sm58 that may have failed due to temp conn errors
- RSARFCDL   Cleans up log file for sm58 transfers
- RSN3_STAT_COLLECTOR- Non R/3 Stat collector
- RSAL_BATCH_TOOL_DISPATCHING - Job for monitoring
- RSN3_AGGR_REORG   Program for Starting the Reorganization Function

37   **We want to introduce MOCD systems in our landscape but we want to know, what are the benefits of MCOD systems?**

MOCD systems in general have following benefits, but there benefits differs as per the customers environment and security policies.

- Flexibility through 'componentization' of systems – each system is independent and therefore can have its own change management and maintenance cycles
- Reduction in the number of database instances - multiple independent and different software solutions are located in one database.
- One logical and physical database instance – for back-up and recovery and from a database administration viewpoint it is one database for operations, tuning and maintenance.
- All systems use the same release for the database – simplified patching and maintenance through standardization.
- Synchronized Disaster Recovery (backup & restore) – One back-up and recovery option for all MCOD systems.
- Separate upgrades possible – each system can be upgraded independently with independent timelines.
- High Scalability/High Availability model for all application must be considered together – since there is a single database, scaling the applications through additional application servers adds additional load on the database and affects all installed applications. Similarly, if the single database is put into a high availability environment, database failover affects all installed applications.
- Independent tuning and administration – from the SAP system perspective, each system can be tuned and maintained independently

38   **We have been thinking to install MCOD systems in our landscape recently, what might be the Administrative constraints for MCOD systems?**

MOCD systems are generally have pros and cons as well, the MCOD configuration does not specifically introduce these challenges as the majority of them also exist for individual systems on dedicated servers.

- Maintenance of multiple applications – Duplicate systems and application administration efforts
- High availability solution costs – each system many need its own High Availability solution and it may entail differing have different levels of High Availability
- Single point of failure for all systems – The database
- CPU/Memory tuning aspects – A holistic view of all systems resource consumption and needs must be considered when tuning the server.
- Database release(s) can impact application release(s) – application upgrades may be restricted based on the database release that must be supported by all application systems

39   **We have been looking towards consolidating our landscape with Virtualization technology so we have been looking towards minimizing the systems in our landscapes, SAP allows us to combine some of the usage types in landscape, what are the benefits of combining the usage types?**

Combining Usage Types and preparation towards consolidation of your Landscape will give below benefits

- A single installation of different but compatible software solutions is located in one database a single system for administration and maintenance.
- One logical and physical database instance – for simplified synchronized back-up and recovery from the DBA viewpoint it is one database for operations tuning and maintenance unlike one system one DB.
- All usage types use the same OS/DB release – simplified tuning, patching and maintenance through standardization on one release/patch set for combined SAP applications Synchronized DR (backup & restore) – One database and SID for automatically synchronized back-ups.
- Simplified Maintenance – one system for change management, one system to patch and one system to upgrade.

- High Scalability/High Availability – Joint protection of critical services bundled in one system is potentially a lower cost as only one High Availability solution needed
- Single tuning and administration – one system to monitor and one system to tune.

Above benefits are solely depends on the customer and policies of the companies and should be considered accordingly.

40   What are the building blocks of effective landscape designing?

During any implementation project designing a system landscape is one of the important and basic tasks. The translation of customer's business process is performed by installing specific group of systems within the landscape.

These building blocks are:

- **Systems with usage types**
    - o   Usage types are realized by installing and configuring a collection of software components. Usage types may also be built on and/or leverage other usage types.

- **Standalone engines**
    - o   Standalone engines are additional software units that are installed separately. Working as a standalone server they provide specific (server) functionality in combination with one or more SAP systems (for example TREX). Standalone engines are not part of a usage type. They do not run on AS ABAP or AS Java and they are never considered to be full-blown SAP NetWeaver systems.

- **Clients**
    - o   Clients are additional installable programs or tools. They either reside on local front-end PCs accessed by users or on back-end systems where they act as client programs within an SAP NetWeaver system landscape

41   We have been learning about Enhanced CTS functionality in SAP Netweaver system can you describe any scenario where Enhanced CTS is useful?

Enhanced CTS functionality is mainly used to transport all types of objects in your production landscape (ABAP as well as Non ABAP)

SAP NetWeaver Exchange Infrastructure (SAP NetWeaver XI) 7.0 SPS14 contains enhanced functionality that enables close coupling between the XI development tools (Integration Repository and Integration Directory) and CTS (Change and Transport System),and enhanced administration support during configuration phase of TMS (Transport Management System) supporting the system maintenance of combined Java and ABAP systems.
You would like to use this features in your SAP NetWeaver XI 7.0 SPS14 systems.

42   We have been hearing about Global Portal and wanted to check the feasibility for this scenario in our Global Landscape, can you elaborate?

Global Portal is a unified SAP portal-based network supporting global organizations, facilitating optimal and seamless runtime access to remote back-end systems, and enhancing content sharing between portals at multiple geographical sites.

The large business enterprises of today are global - serving employees, customers, and an IT infrastructure that is dispersed in numerous geographical locations worldwide. Global Portal network reduces Total Cost of Ownership (TCO) while increasing the autonomy of business units. Sharing content between sites when back-end systems are distributed worldwide improves overall performance, and decreases bandwidth usage.
The advantages of Global Portal are:

- No local installation of IViews is required, meaning reduced downtime for production systems, particularly when new or updated IViews have to be installed

- IViews can be shared by several different portals, enabling departments to share information and applications

- en upgrading to a new version of the portal software, the iViews do not need to be re-installed or re-configured

- e portal becomes interoperable with other portals. In fact, the portal only needs to communicate with other portal interfaces enabling the sharing of different port let technologies including Java, C# and .Net

With the seamless Global Portal and above advantages you can think of implementing in any Global Landscape.

43   **We want to extract archived data from R/3 system. The business content extractor for our respective application does not support the extraction of archived data. Can we get over this situation?**

The scenario is based on the archiving object BC_SBOOK, which is delivered by SAP starting with the R/3 release 4.6B. The method described can be transferred to any other archiving object. We can achieve this with simple steps described as below:

1. Creation of an information structure (T Code SARJ)
2. Creation of the generic DataSource (T Code RSO2)
3. Population of the information structure
An active information structure can be filled by two methods:

- Automatically, when running the deletion program (only applicable for archives filled by the applications – in this case it is advisable to extract the data prior to archiving)

- Manually by the user, since the automatic process is hidden to the end user, and does not require any user interaction (except the scheduling of the deletion job for the archive object).

44   We are recently doing resource budgeting towards our BW implementation project and were wondering what will be the role of responsibility of an SAP BASIS Administrator in our BW implementation project?

There are various activities an SAP BASIS Administrator in the Implementation project, right from planning phase of the project.

- Installation and Planning of BW landscape
- Transport strategy and configuration
- On-going Basis Administration support of SAP R/3 systems.
- Customizing and troubleshooting and day-to-day support.
- SAP security through the profile Generator and Management of Users and Authorizations.
- Logon load balancing
- Data Archiving
- Configuration of operation modes.
- Performance Tuning and Monitoring,
- Lock Management,
- Update Processing,
- View Logs, Short Dumps and Trace Files
- Oracle Database & Table space maintenance
- Workload Analysis
- Performing Client Copy functions
- Batch/Background Jobs Management.
- Support Package administration.
- Backup Management

These are some of the common task as SAP Basis Administrator has to perform.

45   In SAP we have naming conventions for Transport requests can you enlighten us in terms of this naming convention?

In SAP we use Transport requests to transfer the changes to the subsequent systems in production line. SAP has a naming convention towards this transport requests, let's take an example to understand it better:

Transport name consists of 3-letter **system ID**, 1 **letter K** which denotes so called cofile and 6-digit number. In our case CD1 is system ID, K stays unchanged, while 921487 is a transport number so this all constitutes to a Transport request **CD1K921487**

Each time you release a transport requests system creates two files for it, which reside on Application Server. These are:

  cofile - Metadata of a Transport request
  data file - Content of Transport request

Files of these types receive a unique name for each Transport request. They are placed in following directories:

  /usr/sap/trans/cofiles/K<trans_number>.XXX
  /usr/sap/trans/data/R<trans_number>.XXX

Where XXX is our system ID i.e. CD1, PD1, HHD, NSP, EDO etc.

In order we could move our data to external system, all we need is to get those files and copy them on target Application Server. Once it's done, we include those imported objects to a newly created Transport request on destination SAP system.

46   **In our production operations we are facing spool number issues quite frequently, how we can increase or clean the spool numbers for SAP system?**

The Spool is a very important part of your SAP system which is used to print from your SAP system along with monitoring we need to have some maintenance to be done regularly.

Monitoring of your SAP Spool Numbers can be done through SAP CCMS (Tcode RZ20) for all system wide spool servers. We get very useful information about the Spool numbers from here.

• SpoolNumbers - Spool number that is assigned to every output request
• UsedNumbers - Usage of the spool numbers as a percentage

Before we reach 100% on UsedNumbers we should clean up the spool numbers as below:

To clean up SAP Spool Number performs any of the below activity to get rid of the old spool request:

1. Verify the SAP_REORG_SPOOL NEW is executed in SM37. This job will delete the old spool requests and need to be run on daily basis.

2. If the job is not run, you need to manually execute the report RSPO1041 in transaction SE38. Click on execute button and it will delete the old spool requests.

3. Aside to above step, you can delete the old spool request via transaction code SP01. At SP01, list the entire spool request according to the selected date. Click on the recycle bin icon to proceed with the deletions

47   **We are planning to install and SRM system, we would like our suppliers also to use the system outside from our network at the same time we don't want our system to exposed to outside network, what might be the possible solution to this scenario?**

The scenario which we are discussing and trying to implement will be fulfilled by a standalone web dispatcher installation with in the landscape.

SAP Web dispatcher is used for multiple purposes, mainly for URL routing and load balancing. Web dispatcher is exposed to the external world i.e. in internet, it is very important to use secure protocol connections.

The SAP Web dispatcher lies between the Internet and our SAP system. It is the entry point for HTTP(s) or http requests into your system, which consists of one or more Netweaver application servers. SAP Web dispatcher can reject or accept connections. When it accepts a connection, it balances the load to ensure an even distribution across the servers. The SAP Web Dispatcher therefore contributes to security and also balances the load in our SAP system.

The web browser communicates with the SAP Web Dispatcher via an SSL secured http communication (https). The SSL encryption will be terminated at the SAP Web Dispatcher and will be forwarded without SSL encryption to the SAP WebAS via http.

We can install standalone SAP Webdispatcher with the help of sapinst.

48   We would like to know something about the parameter configuration regarding to SNC, can you please describe some of the important parameters?

The common scenario for using SNC with your to secure gateway.
There are a number of parameters that control the behaviour of the SAP Gateway in conjunction with SNC (Secure Network Communication).

snc/enable

This parameter specifies whether the gateway accepts connections that protect the data via SNC.

snc/permit_insecure_comm

This parameter specifies whether the gateway accepts connections without SNC

snc/permit_insecure_start

This parameter specifies whether the gateway may establish connections with programs that communicate without SNC.

snc/permit_common_name

This parameter specifies whether the gateway can use a default SNC name specified by the parameter snc/identity/as, if an SNC name for the connection cannot be read from `secinfo`.

snc/gssapi_lib

This parameter specifies path for shared library of the security system in use.

snc/identity/as

Identity of the gateway application server

49   In recent years SAP has advised all customers that they have stopped development of SM36 and SM37 do you have any comment on this?

Yes SAP has stopped further development of T codes SM36 and SM37 which we use commonly for background job administration in SAP system.

SAP have been introducing a job scheduling mgmt. tool called SAP CPS which has more dynamic functionalities and event driven approach towards job scheduling mgmt. for an SAP System.

50   What is the difference between proxies and adapters?

Proxies are nothing but interfaces, which will get executcd in the application system. They can be created only in the system from message interfaces using the proxy generation functions. You can use proxies for systems with WAS >=6.20.

Adapters will convert one format into another expected/target format. means from SAP standard formats and as well as 3rd party formats to target formats

51   Can we discuss about architecture of Oracle Database? What are the main
        components and what exactly their function and importance?

Architecture of Oracle is pretty simple and provides a very clear view as far as functionality is concerned.

Oracle Listener: Oracle listener facilitates the communication between clients and Oracle instance. To be very precise Oracle Listener is not actually part of the architecture of database but it's a part of Networking process which works with Oracle.

Oracle Process : Oracle process aka Shadow process with SAP are 1:1 connected with SAP work processes, whenever a database request comes towards Database from SAP work process, Listener creates a shadow workprocess at database level to facilitate the requests from SAP.

Oracle Buffers: Database is always stored in data files, to perform faster read and write operation of the database, Oracle database has its own buffer in SYSTEM GLOBAL AREA (SGA).
Shared cursor cache is used for storing SQL statements executed on DB and row cache holds data dictionary information of Oracle.

Data Files: Data files are nothing but the files which actually holds the data at disk level.

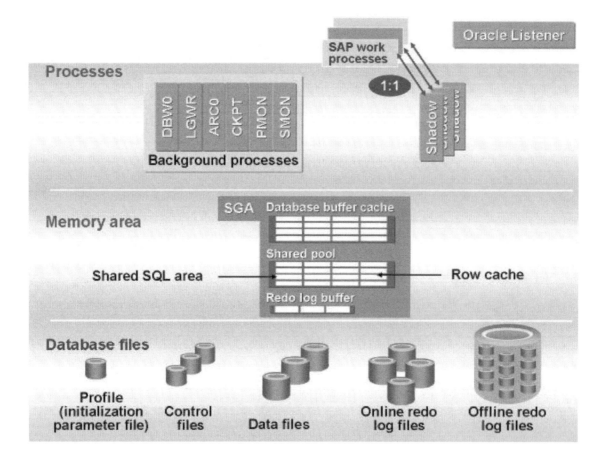

52 We have been hitting with checkpointer issues recently for our Database, can you explain in detail how does this exactly work at DB level.

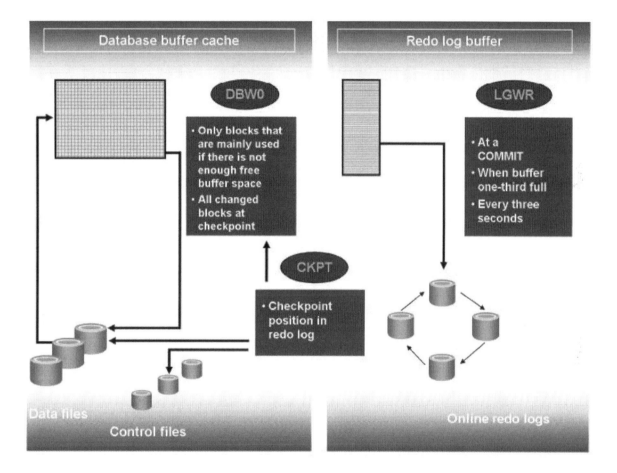

Checkpoint in Oracle points to mainly two events,

- Checkpoint is the point where database writer moves all changed buffers from memory to DB files.
- Checkpoint is the point in redo log files, it's the point where we can recover database consistently in case of failures. It serves as a consistent state point of DB.

There is a process called CKTP at DB level which actually performs all checkpoint operations on DB.

- It writes checkpoint information to data file header
- It writes information about checkpoint position in online redo log files to control file.

Frequency of the checkpoint is always critical to decide because actually it decides the time required for instance to recover from failure.

We can provide checkpoint frequency via oracle parameters but in SAP we generally make use of log switch event only for checkpoint frequency.

53   What are some of the common Oracle Database environment variables in windows environment?

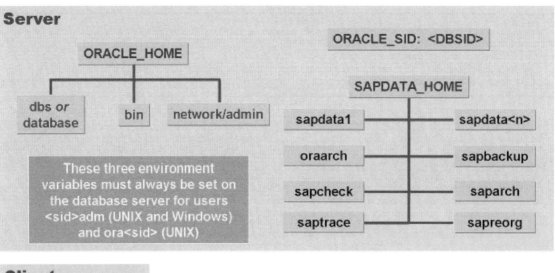

ORACLE_SID: System ID of Database in SAP system

ORACLE_HOME: This is the location of the Oracle Software, these variable points specifically to subdirectories like bin, network & dbs.

SAPDATA_HOME: Directory in which all datafiles are stored at os level.

54   Can you details the DBA planning calendar?

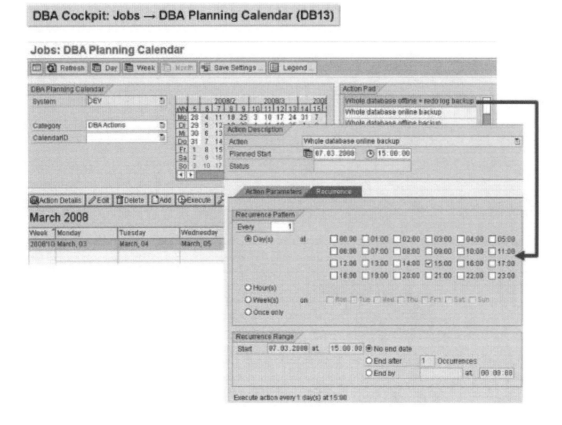

DB13 – DBA planning calendar is a central tool for almost all important activities we perform on Database lever

- Online Database Backup
- Offline Database Backup
- Offline + Redo Backup
- Update Optimizer statistics
- RUNSTAT for tables and indexes

All the database backup and configuration of scheduled activities is done through DB13 – DBA Planning calendar.

55 **Can we detail a bit about how an SAP ABAP+JAVA system starts? The sequences in exact and details about the steps as well:**

1. To start an SAP system there are several ways and tools can be used in current SAP Environment. We take a traditional way of doing it via logging on to OS level and executing startsap command

2. Issues a startsap Command

3. The database instance was checked and if not DB instance is started first

4. The central services instance of SAP system then started in case of ABAP+JAVA and JAVA Only systems

5. The Central instance for ABAP is started

6. Then ABAP Dispatcher of ABAP instance invokes startup and control framework for JAVA and start the JAVA instance in turn

7. If there is any Dialog instance, the startup of the dialog instance started

8. The Dialog instance ABAP dispatcher in turn invoke Dialog JAVA instance

9. Dialog JAVA instance started

This is a general procedure how and SAP ABAP + JAVA system starts

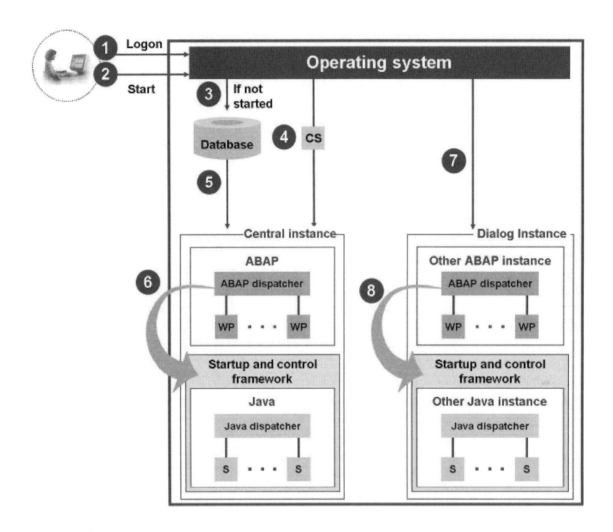

56   In our current Landscape we would like to use a web based tool for starting stopping
        of our SAP systems to our level 1 support, our main purpose is to restrict the login to
        OS level just for starting and stopping.

SAP has introduced SAP Management Console which suits exactly to this situation and we can now
manage our SAP systems thorough a web based access to management console.

http://<hostname>:5<instancenumber>13

Even this access is given to https secured connections also

https://<hostname>:5<instancenumber>14

The SAP MC is supplied as standard with the start program sapstartsrv and is ready for use without any additional installation

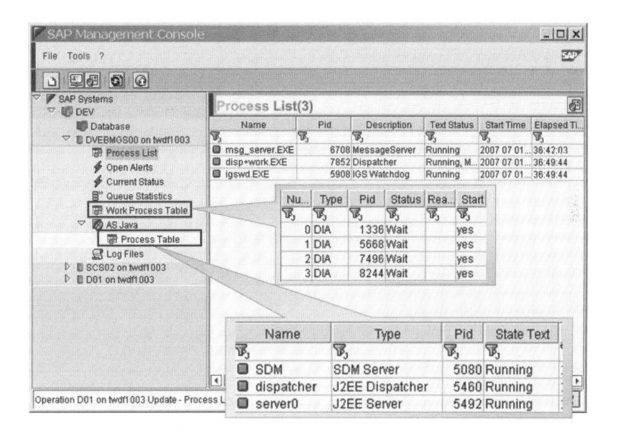

The SAP MC allows you to start and stop all the SAP NetWeaver AS ABAP + Java instances as well as the Central Services. You can also display information about the instances of the SAP system and the corresponding database (name, manufacturer and name of the host on which the database is located).

57   One of our Java instance is restarting automatically after hours of operations and we have investigated the issue with SAP and they asked us to change the VM settings for our java instance. Where can we change the VM settings of our Java Instance?

VM settings (Virtual Memory) settings of your java instance are one of the important settings to keep your all java applications running. Due to the nature of the Java applications they require some more memory.

The VM settings of Java Instance can be changed through tool called Configtool which is located at OS level at **\usr\sap\<SID>\<central instance>\j2ee\configtool.**

Click on the instance for which you want to change the VM settings and in the right hand panel you can see the VM parameters for that particular instance. Make the required changes and save. You will need to restart your instance to make these VM parameters effective.

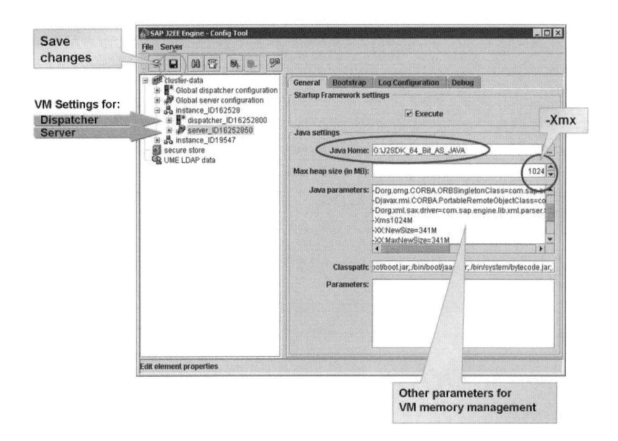

58   Please describe the procedure to implement patch using JSPM for SAP Netweaver Java system.

We patch all the java components of an SAP system with a tool called JSPM (Java Support Package Manager); the procedure to update the software components is as below:

Prerequisites

- The AS Java and the database have been backed up.
- The support packages you want to apply have been downloaded to the global EPS inbox directory /usr/sap/trans/EPS/in....
- The <SID>adm user has Read permissions for the global EPS inbox directory usr/sap/trans/EPS/in.
- There is enough disk space.

Procedure

- Choose the Deployment tab.
- Select the Package Type (Single Support Packages)
- All the available software components from your system which can be patched will be shown.

Specify the Queue

You can specify which software components you want to update and to which patch level and define the queue. JSPM automatically check all the required files from inbox and show the status of the files which can be deployed.

Deploy Queue

JSPM starts the deployment of the software components that you selected. The status of all software components changes to SCHEDULED.

If you have selected to update the kernel, and if your system is distributed, during the deployment you are first prompted to stop the primary application server instance and any running dialog instances, and to choose Next.

Then you are prompted to start the primary application server instance and to choose Next.

Completed

Check the logs for any errors.

59 With our Netweaver 7.1 system we have a New SAP NWA tool, we would like to know the details about the tool and weather it is capable of starting and stopping on SAP system?

SAP NetWeaver Administrator (SAP NWA) is a new tool for administration and monitoring. The SAP NWA combines the most important administration and monitoring tools for Java in a new, browser-bases user interface.

It provides functions in a wide variety of areas (monitoring, configuration, administration, performance analysis). In the administration area, you will find plug-ins for user administration, for applications and for systems.

We can invoke the SAP NWA using the URL: http://<Host>:<Port>/nwa

Administration tab in the NWA used:

The "Administration" area in the NWA contains areas for system and application administration as well as for user management.

- Starting and stopping instances (see figure: SAP NWA: System Administration).
- Starting and stopping cluster elements (dispatcher, server, SDM)
- Starting and stopping applications

60   With some of our Java applications we are facing performance issues, we would like to add server process to some of our application servers, and how we can do this?

Adding a server process in Java Application servers is done with the help of configtool. select an instance or a node of an instance, the Add server button, with which you can add an additional server process, becomes active. See the figure "Server Processes: Add"

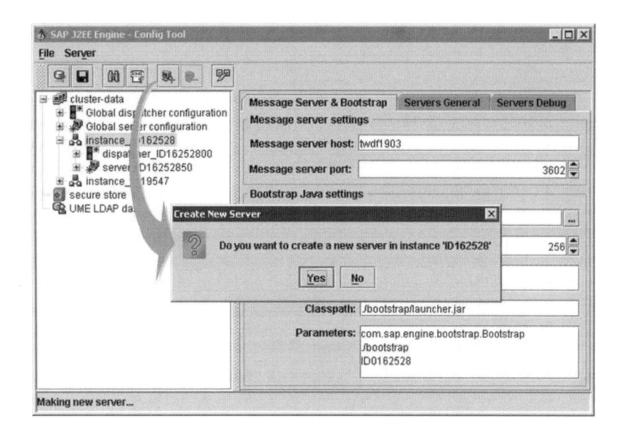

Before the new server process is added, a popup appears with a confirmation prompt.

The join-Port is usually composed of 5<instance number><20+5*(number of the server process). In the example, this is 5<21><20+5*1> = 52125.

61 We are planning to Setup SSL communications in out landscape; can you describe the roadmap to setup SSL in SAP Landscape?

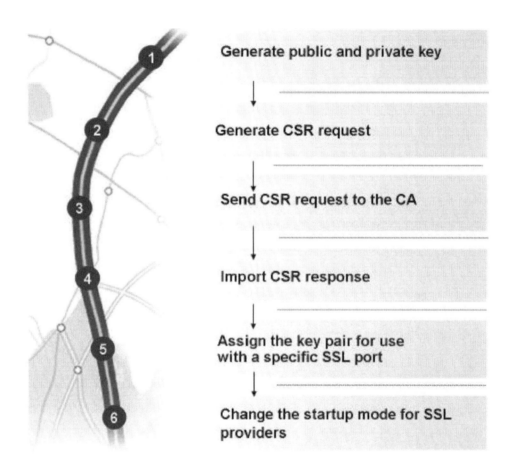

There is a simple roadmap to setup SSL in your landscape,

- Generate Public and Private Key

- The basis of SSL is cryptography; SAP NetWeaver Application Server Java has to be enabled in order to support this feature. This cryptographic software is already delivered with SAP NetWeaver AS Java installation.

- Generate CSR Request

  - Certificate Signing request have to generate signing from the certificate Authority

- Send CSR Request

  - Send SCR request to Certification Authority eg SAP OSS, follow the instructions given at SAP Trust Center Service service.sap.com/tcs

- Import CSR Response

  - Import Certificate response from Trust Center service in SAP Java.

- Assign the ports to the Key Pairs

  - Assign the SSL Ports in SSL settings for your SAP Java and restart the server

62   **Describe the complete SSL Server authentication Process:**

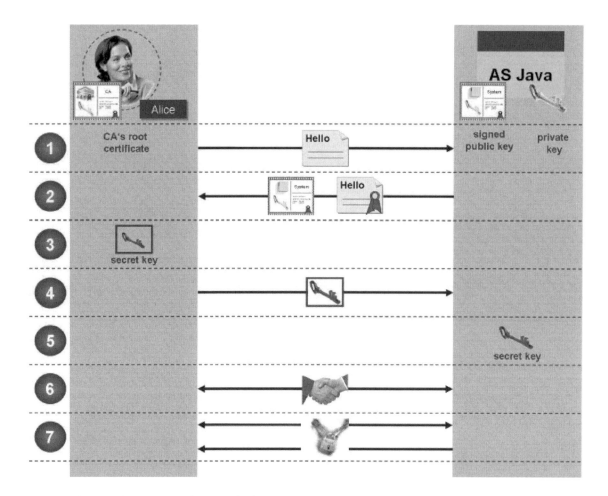

The complete authentication flows as below:

- User contacts the SAP NetWeaver Application Server Java using a client's web browser
- The Application Server responds and sends its Public Key with a digitally-signed message.
- The Secret Key is created and encrypted with the Public Key the server sent before
- The client sends back the encrypted Secret Key
- On the server the Secret Key is decrypted using the Private Key. Only the server can decrypt the received Secret Key because it's holding the Private Key which is necessary for the decrypting.
- The communication partners perform a Handshake".
- Further communication between the client and the server is encrypted using the Secret Key

63   We are planning our ECC 5.0 Landscape upgrade to newest version of ECC, during the planning phase we have encountered the phase where we need to decide on the modification adjustments and the no of objects involved, can we have some details what actually it meant for?

During the day to day operations of the SAP systems we always need to have additional modification to the system Repository through Customer developments. In the SAP system, you can create your own Repository objects, such as tables, programs, transactions, and so on. All customer development normally takes place in the customer namespace, that is, all the objects created by the customer have names from a specified namespace; these names generally start with the letters Y or Z. This applies to ABAP programs, tables and so on. SAP has also provided its customers with an additional method of globally unique assignment of individual namespaces for several years. Such a customer namespace could be, for example, /<companyname>/.

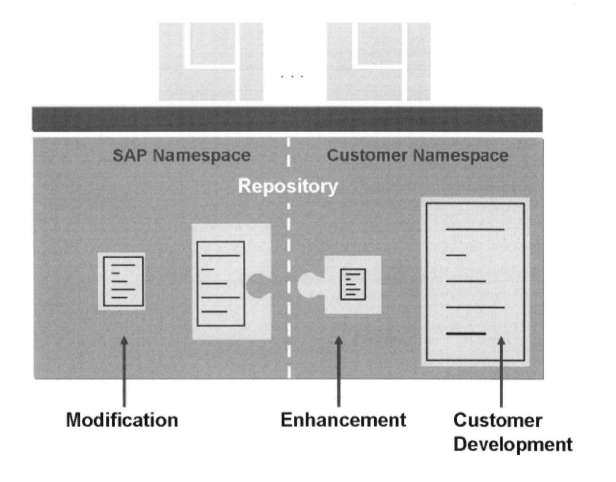

Another type of Changing the Repository through enhancements: In this type of change, you add customer-specific objects to the Repository. There are specific places in the coding, known as customer exits, where you can supplement the SAP standard system with your own objects. There is also another modern method for the customer-specific enhancement of the standard: the use of so-called Business Add-Ins (BAdIs).

Last and one of the important type Modifications to the standard SAP system: Changes to SAP objects such as programs and table definitions are called modifications. The Repository delivered by SAP is not only extended, but changed. When you next upgrade your system or when importing Support Packages, you will therefore need to check these modifications against the new Repository.

During the upgrade the upgrade time is directly in relation with the objects in modification type where we have changed SAP delivered objects and the changes we want to keep or let upgrade program overwrite is the decision we have to take.

64   What is SMICM used for and what are its capabilities in terms of Internet Communication Framework?

With introduction of ICM (Internet Communication Manager) in Netweaver we have lot of scalability and flexibility in terms of web connectivity to SAP Systems

The T Code SMICM used for monitoring and administering ICM in SAP ABAP system. Some of capable functions are as below:

- Monitoring and restarting the ICM

- Configuring the trace level (*Goto* → *Trace Level* → ...), values from 0 to 3.

- Evaluating the trace files (*Goto* → *Trace File* → ...); the system reads the *dev_icm* file from the *work* directory of the current instance.

- Overview of the profile parameters (*Goto* → *Parameters* → *Display/Change*).

- The ICM is configured using profile parameters. The displayed values apply for the instance to which you are currently logged on. For documentation on the parameters, see the ICM monitor (*Goto* → *Parameters* → *Change* and choose *Documentation*), transaction RZ11, and SAP Library.

- Display the statistics (*Goto* → *Statistics* → *Display*). You can use these statistics to find out how many requests the ICM has processed since it was started (or since the statistics were reset). The system also displays information about processing duration.

- Monitoring (*Goto* → *HTTP Server Cache* → *Display*) and resetting (*Goto* → *HTTP Server Cache* → *Invalidate* → ...) the ICM server cache. The ICM server cache stores HTTP objects before they are sent to the client. The next time that this object is requested, the content can be sent directly from the cache to the client.

- In maintenance mode, the ICM log off from the ABAP message server and is not available for Web requests. The ICM processes only the remaining requests. If an Internet user accesses an ICM in this status from the browser, the system issues a message stating that the ICM is in .Maintenance Mode.

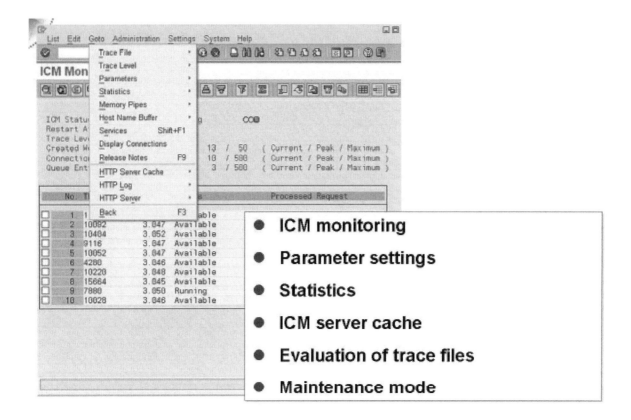

65   Can you describe a more about worker thread of ICM and all other components in
      ICM?

From a technical point of view, the ICM is a separate process (*icman* at operating system level) that is
started and monitored by the ABAP dispatcher. Its task is to ensure that the SAP system can
communicate with the outside world (using HTTP, HTTPS, and SMTP). In the server role, it can process
requests from the Internet that arrive with URLs with the server/port combination for which the ICM is
listening.

The ICM then calls the appropriate local handler, depending on the URL. The ICM process uses threads
to process the created workload in parallel. The components of the ICM are:

- **Thread Control**: This thread accepts the incoming TCP/IP requests and creates (or rises) a
  worker thread from the thread pool to process the request.

- **Worker Thread**: This thread handles requests and responses for a connection. A worker thread contains an I/O handler for the network input and output, and various plug-ins for the different supported protocols.

- **Watchdog**: A worker thread usually waits for a response (whether it is client or server); if a timeout occurs, the watchdog takes over the task of waiting for the response. The worker thread can then be used for other requests.

- **Signal Handler**: Processes signals that are sent from the operating system or another process (such as the ABAP dispatcher).

- **Connection Info**: Table with information for each existing network connection.

- **Memory Pipes**: These memory-based communication objects allow data transfer between the ICM and the ABAP work processes.

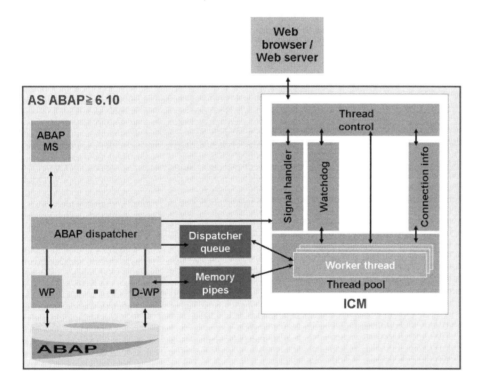

66   **We have been using our SAP Landscape since long now, and due to enhanced functionalities with Netweaver version we would like to have some of our applications to be accessed outside network, but at the same time we are worried about security of our systems in such scenarios, how can we achieve this with safest possible solution.**

There are several third party products we can use in such kind of scenarios like Reverse Proxies, Web switches, etc., but one of the stable and cost effective solutions to these scenarios would be to use SAP Web Dispatcher.

The SAP Web Dispatcher, acts like a software Web switch. It is a stand-alone program that you can run on a separate host without any additional software. In this way, the SAP Web Dispatcher implements a central entry point for HTTP(S) requests to an SAP system, including load distribution across multiple instances.

An HTTP request is assigned to a server in two stages:

1. SAP Web Dispatcher determines whether the incoming HTTP request is to be forwarded to an ABAP or Java server. It then finds a group of servers in the SAP system that can execute the request.

2. Load balancing is then carried out within this group. After the SAP Web Dispatcher has identified a server, it forwards the request to the ICM of the relevant application server.

In such a way we can achieve an effective solution in DMZ (De Militarized Zone) without exposing your SAP Landscape to outside network in terms provides you the topmost security with effective solution.

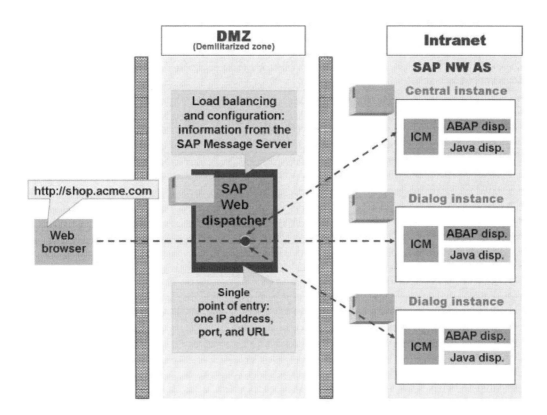

67   **What are the load balancing scenarios available for customers as of SAP Netweaver AS?**

There are mainly two types of Load balancing Scenarios available for customers below are some pros and cons for these scenarios:

Server Based Load Balancing:

A load balancer connected in front acts as a central entry point to the SAP system. This is the case, even if the SAP system is made up of multiple application servers. This technique offers the following advantages:

- All application servers can be addressed using a common IP address or a common name.
- The users always use the same URL to access the system.
- One SSL server certificate is sufficient for all of the application servers.
- The advantages listed above reduce the operating and maintenance effort and costs.

Client Based Load Balancing

With client-based load balancing, all inbound client requests are initially directed to a central location in the system, a load balancing server, when the connection is first made. The load balancing server informs the client which application server it should address.

Some of the disadvantages of the Client based load balancing are as following:

- Can lead to confusion of the user, since the URL displayed in the browser changes with the rerouting
- If Favourites are created in the browser, these point to the server to which the user was rerouted
- Each application server requires a server certificate
- Can cause problems if a firewall is used

68   What are the different types of Users in SAP Systems?

Dialog

A normal *dialog* user is used for all logon types by just one person. During a dialog logon, the system checks for expired/initial passwords, and the user has the opportunity to change own password. Multiple dialog logons are checked and, if appropriate, logged.

System

Use the *System* user type for dialog-free communication within a system or for background processing within a system, or also for RFC users for various applications, such as ALE, Workflow, Transport Management System, and Central User Administration. It is not possible to use this type of user for a dialog logon.

Communication

Use the *communication* user type for dialog-free communication between systems. It is not possible to use this type of user for a dialog logon. The usual settings for the validity period of a password apply to users of this type.

Service

A user of the type *Service* is a dialog user that is available to a larger, anonymous group of users. In general, you should only assign highly restricted authorizations to users of this type. Service users are used, for example, for anonymous system accesses using an ITS or ICF service.

Reference

Like the service user, a *reference* user is a general non-person-related user. You cannot use a reference user to log on. A reference user is used only to assign additional authorizations. You can specify a reference user for a dialog user for additional authorization on the *Roles* tab page.

69   In the Authorization concept of SAP, how can we manually change and maintain the authorization data for particular transaction codes of Authorization objects?

There are several situations during the implementation of SAP system, where we need to adjust the authorizations to several critical data in our SAP systems.

Role maintenance T Code PFCG can be used to automatically create the authorizations that are associated with the transactions specified in the menu tree. But there are several requirements where we need to adjust the values in accordance with the actual requirements and authorities.

Choose the Authorizations tab page and then Display Authorization Data or Change Authorization Data, depending on the maintenance mode. Check the scope and contents of the authorizations.

If these are proposed by the system, a **green traffic light** in the authorization overview indicates that role maintenance has supplied at least one proposal for each authorization field. A **yellow traffic light** indicates that the authorization must be maintained manually after it has been created. Role maintenance does not provide a default value for the authorization.

A **red traffic light** therefore indicates an unmaintained organizational level.

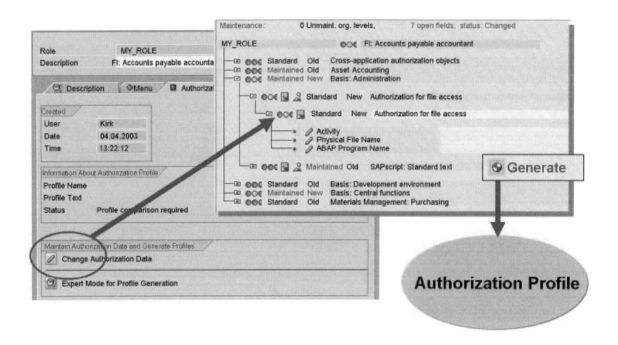

70   There are several things related to Users we would like to review, for example what
      are the changes made to certain user's authorizations recently? When did the last log
      on for the specific user? Where we can get such comprehensive information towards
      users and authorizations in SAP?

There is a central information repository in SAP system called Information System T Code SUIM where
we can get all the information related to user activities and Roles & Authorizations related changes to
his usermaster records, we can get all information related to Roles and authorizations as well, some of
the common questions we can answer are as below:

- Which users have been locked in the system by administrators or failed logon attempts?
- When did a user last log on to the system?
- What changes were made in the authorization profile of a user?
- In which roles is a certain transaction contained?
- When the user was locked and how?
- How many users which have certain imp authorizations in System?
- How many roles we have for certain t Code?

This all information is useful to do a sanity check on the user and authorization concept and prepare some of the important reports for SAP Security Audit.

71   We have several SAP systems in our Landscape with multiple clients in systems for designated purposes; we have been looking towards an easy user administration tool which we can use in all SAP systems?

User administration is a critical and time consuming process when it comes to multiple systems with multiple clients, SAP has provided a tool called Central User Administration to facilitate the user administration.

Identical users are created a number of times in different clients; you can significantly reduce your administrative effort for user administration using Central User Administration (CUA). We can perform user maintenance centrally from one client with CUA. This client is then described as the central system. The clients for which user administration is performed from the central system are called child systems. We can specify for every user which clients it can log on to. Using CUA does not mean that all users can be used in all clients of the system landscape. We can also specify which user data can only be maintained centrally and which data can also be maintained locally. It is sometimes useful to allow data to be locally maintained by the users or by an administrator. Local maintenance with distribution to all other clients is also possible.

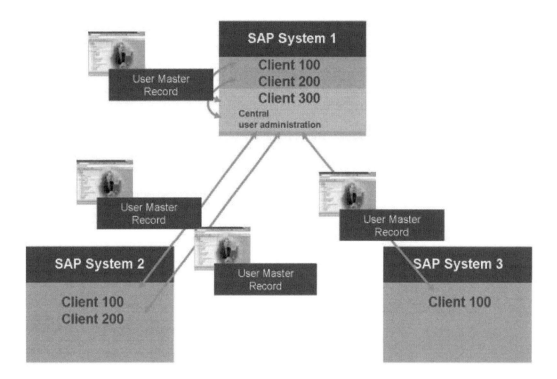

72   We are in middle of planning of our landscape including Java systems and we want our Java systems to be configured for our ABAP systems, we need to change our some of existing systems also to point from JAVA UME to ABAP, what are the possible options to change the UME datastore?

While deciding to switch the existing datasources there are some restrictions as below:

- **System database (*dataSourceConfiguration_database_only.xml*):** You can switch to any arbitrary LDAP configuration file (*dataSourceConfiguration_[ldap description]_db.xml*) or an ABAP system (*dataSourceConfiguration_abap.xml*). In this case, you must make sure that the new data source does not contain any users and groups with the same unique attributes as the database (i.e. the new data source must not contain any users or groups with the same unique name or ID as the users or groups in the database).

- **ABAP system (*dataSourceConfiguration_abap.xml*):** No change is possible.
- **Directory service (*dataSourceConfiguration_[ldap description]_db.xml*):** If you have selected an LDAP directory as the user data source, you can modify the structure of the LDAP directory or switch to a different LDAP if this does not modify any unique user IDs.

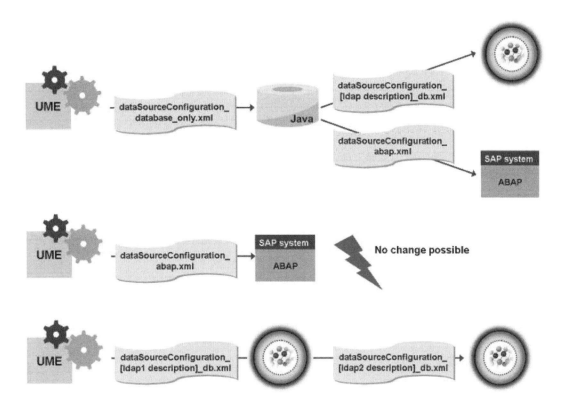

73   We are planning to change the existing datasources of one of our SAP JAVA system; we want to know the process of changing the existing datasource for our JAVA UME?

Changing an existing data source can be done with the help of Configtool, here we can display and change the datasource, process goes as follows:

As this is one of the advanced settings for your JAVA Stack, it can only be made in Offline Configuration Editor mode:

1. Stop all the Java instances of you system

2. Start the Configuration Tool

3. Switch to Offline Configuration Editor Mode

4. Switch to change mode.

5. Navigate to *cluster_data* → *server* → *cfg* → *services* → *Propertysheet*

com.sap.security.core.ume.service

6. Make the required changes (*Apply Custom*)

7. Start your system's Java instances

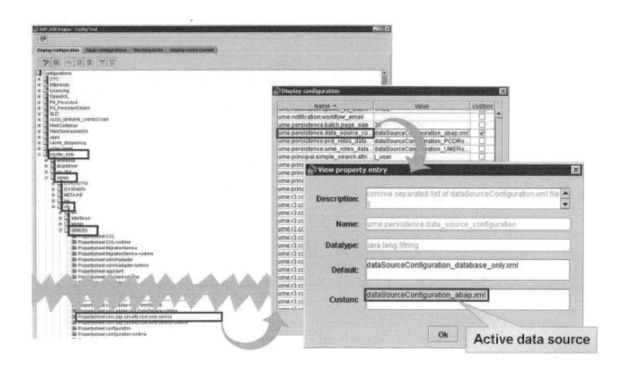

74   We have been looking towards a JAVA Authorization concept and we understand a
      significance change in the way we gather authorizations in JAVA stack, can you details
      a bit?

In JAVA with ABAP as a datasource have significant advancement in authorization concept, users from
ABAP systems need special authorization for JAVA stack, and there are some applications which need

authorization from ABAP stack. The ABAP roles have been represent as groups in JAVA stack, so whenever we assign any role in JAVA with JAVA groups ABAP authorizations are also included.

So bottom line is we have JAVA groups represented from an ABAP Role. This eliminates the overhead of creating and assigning the respective roles twice in the ABAP and JAVA systems.

The Groups from ABAP will be automatically added to the user authorizations in JAVA side.

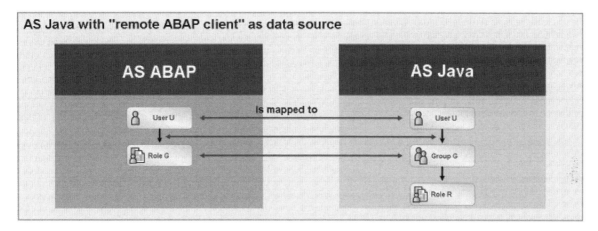

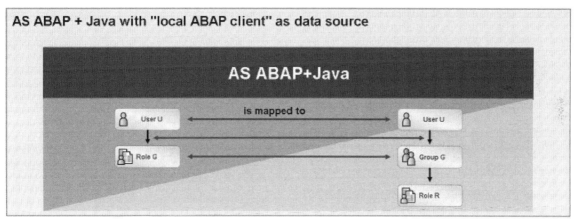

75 **We are experiencing a huge load on some of our servers, even though there are more servers which are less utilized by the end users. We have to streamline this server usage so that all servers should be used for better performance, how we can achieve this?**

These situations are likely to occur if we don't use SAP Logon Load Balancing feature provided by SAP. With Logon Load Balancing we can distribute all end users to available application servers. We can create logon groups as below:

2. We can create Logon groups with T code SMLG

3. In the Create/Change Entry dialog box, you can configure the following options:

   o Group assignment: The Name of the logon Group
   o Instance: Select the application server to be added to this group, for adding multiple application servers we have to perform above step repeatedly.
   o Response time: Specify the Response time for the application servers for this logon groups and system automatically sets a homogeneous value for all groups that are associated with that instance.
   o Users: The maximum number of configured users who can be logged on to an instance.

Save entries and your Logon group is ready to be used.

76   What is the concept of J2ee Security Roles and how it has been implemented with JAVA Stack of SAP Netweaver?

J2EE security roles allow an access check for J2EE applications. The authorizations are defined declaratively. A developer creates a J2EE security role for each new application object. These objects are consolidated during the assembly process and made available on the J2EE server. A user can use these objects only if the administrator has specified the user or group name in the J2EE security role.

We can use Visual Administrator to assign security role to a user or group. A J2EE security role can be assigned

- either directly to users and/or groups
- or as a so-called reference role to precisely one J2EE security role in the component *SAP-J2EE-Engine*

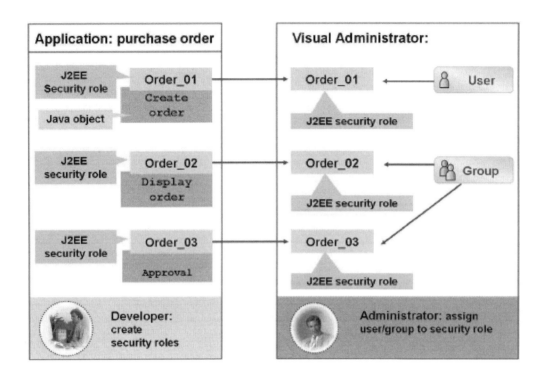

77   A J2ee Security Role has been created by one of our developer and applications has
         been deployed on one of our JAVA Stack, we would like to give authorizations to one
         of our tester to test the application before we move it to our Production server, how
         we can assign the j2ee Security role to our tester?

With the application development, developers create all the access roles to the application in the form
of .xml file and we can use these access roles in visual administrator as j2ee security roles.

To assign security roles, proceed as follows:

1. Start the Visual Administrator (\usr\sap\<SID>\<instance>\j2ee\admin\go).

2. Navigate to *Server* → *Services* → *Security Provider* → *Runtime* → *Policy Configurations*.

3. In the *Components* area, select the application (or service).

4. Choose the *Security Roles* tab page.

5. In the *Security Roles* area, select the security role that you want to assign.

6. Switch to change mode if necessary.

7. Depending on the type of J2EE security role, you either

- perform assignment directly to users and/or groups

- perform assignment to a reference security role

78   What are the Ume Roles and how they are better than J2ee Security Roles?

In most of the implementations of JAVA authorizations we use UME roles, UME roles are easy to manage and scalable unlike j2ee Security Roles, we can combine different actions in one Role which we cannot achieve with J2ee Security Roles.

The authorization concept in the UME uses permissions, actions, and roles.

Permissions are defined in the Java coding. This is known as programmable security. Permissions are used to provide an access control. Permissions cannot be assigned directly to a user.

An **action** is a collection of permissions. A Java application defines its own actions and specifies the authorizations in an XML file *<name of the application>.xml.*

Actions are displayed in the UME Administration Console. You can use the UME Administration Console to combine these actions into **roles**.

UME roles group actions of one or more applications. You can assign UME roles to users in the UME Administration Console.

SAP's Java applications work with UME roles. If SAP delivers a WebDynpro application, you can only assign authorizations using UME roles.

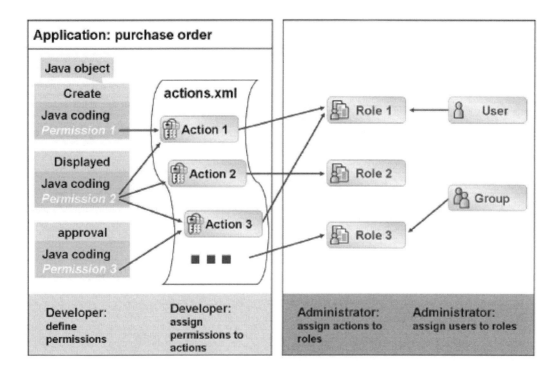

79   As a service provider the situations comes very often that we forget the Java administrator user's password and we need to rest the password, what are the implications of this process?

The administrator user can be used be person who is a system administrator and there is several internal usage of the administrator use in Java stack.

If the SDM server performs deployment (e.g. when customer developments are imported via the NWDI or corrections with the JSPM) then it requires an administration user. It is only possible to log onto the SDM server via the SDM password. In addition, the SDM server cannot read any password information from the system database's Java schema. To do this, the SDM server accesses **secure storage** which is implemented as a file in the file system. This contains among other things the user and password of the *single* administration user.

Whenever we change the administrator user password we need to update the password in secure store as well, this we can do with configtool only.

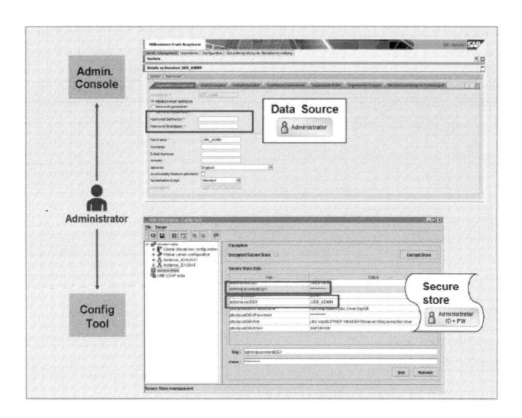

80   **We have recently performing the maintenance of our systems and accidently we have locked all the users of JAVA Stack and now we cannot enter into our JAVA Stack, any solution to this?**

This kind of situation can occur into any landscape where we accidently lock or incorrectly configure UME for any JAVA Stack.

SAP has provided a user SAP* which can come to rescue in this situation, SAP* is a powerful user with which we can login to any application or configuration of JAVA Stack. For security reasons we need to activate this user and set a temporary password to it.

Proceed as follows to make a correction with the *SAP*￼* user:

1. Activate the *SAP*￼* user

 a) Stop the Java cluster.

 b) In the Configtool, open the Configuration Editor mode.

 c) Navigate to *cluster_data* → *Server* → *cfg* → *services* → *Propertysheet*

 com.sap.security.core.ume.service

 d) Switch to change mode.

 e) Set *ume.superadmin.activated* to the value **true**. Set *ume.superadmin.password* to any password.

 f) Start the Java cluster.

2. Change the configuration

 a) Log on with the user **SAP*** and the password that you have just set

 b) Correct the problem; for example, unlock the administration user

3. Deactivate the *SAP*￼* user

 a) Stop the Java cluster.

 b) In the Configtool, open the Configuration Editor mode.

 c) Navigate to *cluster_data* → *Server* → *cfg* → *services* → *Propertysheet*

 com.sap.security.core.ume.service

 d) Switch to change mode.

 e) Set *ume.superadmin.activated* to the value **false**.

 f) Start the Java cluster.

81 **We have central monitoring system configured in our landscape, we were wondering if we plan to shift this functionality to a dedicated server due to server load, how actually it works internally so that we can plan to shift this system?**

CCMS infrastructure is so matured enough now it can handle SAP as well as non-SAP components for central monitoring also, the infrastructure must be installed on every component that is to be centrally monitored. This is automatically the case for SAP systems with software component SAP_BASIS 4.0 or above. SAP R/3 3.x systems and components on which no SAP system is active are connected using CCMS agents.

Each component collects its own monitoring data using the infrastructure and stores it locally in the main memory. This part of the main memory is called the **monitoring segment**. Its size can be configured.

The central monitoring system collects the monitoring data for the components and displays it in various views. In this way, the administrator has a central view of the entire system landscape.

So while thinking to move this system to a dedicated server, it should have as high a release level as possible and also be highly available.

In large system landscapes, it is recommended that you include a separate system that is used only for special tasks such as central monitoring, Central User Administration, transport domains controller, or the SAP Solution Manager. From a performance point of view, the workload of the central monitoring system increases only insignificantly, as the collection of monitoring data is usually decentralized.

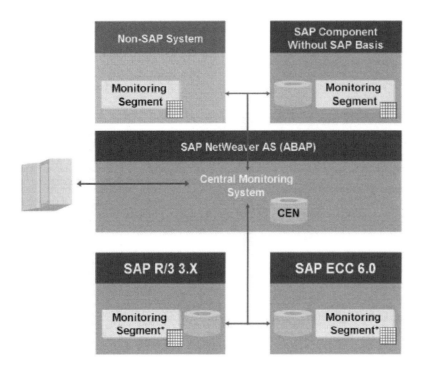

82   **We want to minimize alert emails from our Central monitoring system during night time, so we would like to have different thresholds at different time, can we achieve this?**

We can use the properties variants to control the situation of unwanted alerts at night time; it can store the threshold values in containers and activate them as necessary.

Properties variants have three advantages:

- We can manually switch from one properties variant to another for test purposes or to adjust the monitor to a special situation. This means that all monitor settings are automatically changed in accordance with the current properties variant.

- We can connect a properties variant to an operation mode. In this way, the threshold value (for a yellow alarm) for the dialog response time is set to 1400ms during the day, while the threshold value is automatically increased to 3500ms after the switch to night operation, since there is usually no dialog processing in your monitored system during the night.

- We can transport the contents of properties variants to other SAP systems using the transport system. For example, if you create a variant for production systems in the central monitoring system, and define the threshold values that are to apply for production systems there, you can then transport the variant to all production systems and activate the threshold values there.

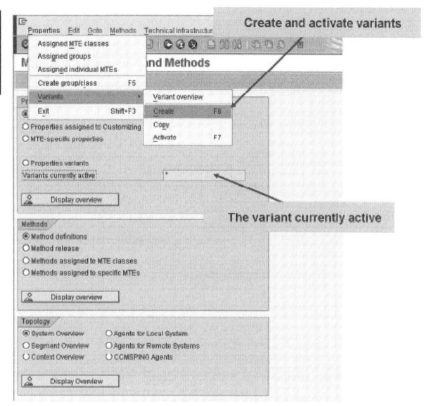

83   We have been looking towards standard monitoring tools for our SAP JAVA Netweaver stack for quite some time now and we were wondering if we can create our own tool to monitor our JAVA application the way we want?

SAP uses JMX architecture to monitor the JAVA component of SAP; there are several tasks of JMX infrastructure:

- Monitoring the current status
- Creating a history
- Using an alert mechanism to react to critical situations

The JMX infrastructure is provided by the *JMX Adapter* service. Since JMX is a standard, this ensures that external tools can also access the monitoring data. The external tools connect through the JMX API and can display all current values in the JMX monitors. They can also create, delete, and change groups, as well as installing and uninstalling monitor nodes.

The data collection is performed at runtime. For this, the data can either be periodically fetched from the JMX monitors (passive), or the resources themselves send the data to the JMX monitors using event mechanisms (active). When the SAP NetWeaver AS Java is started, the JMX monitors are created, and are provided with data at runtime.

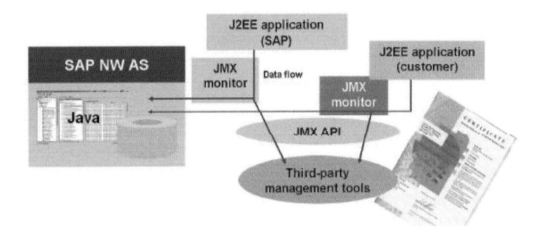

84   For central monitoring system we need to add out JAVA stack can you detail a bit about registering agent for JAVA?

For adding java system in your central monitoring system we need to register CCMSR agent in visual administrator,

Visual Administrator on the dispatcher node select monitoring segment:
Select monitoring conf file and register.

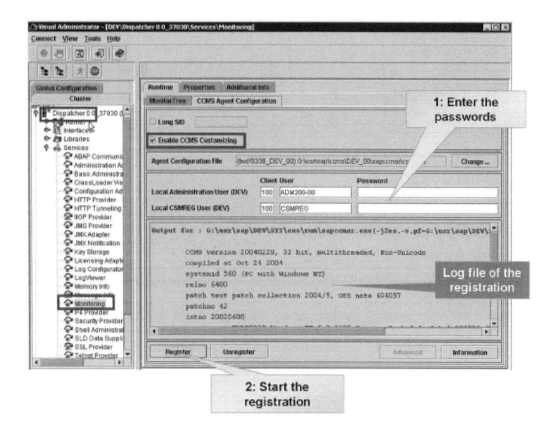

85   We have several mission critical applications on our JAVA stack, and we are very
        much concerned about these applications availability, we would like to know how to
        keep our support team more alerted about these applications status?

In Java we have the GRMG infrastructure to support this kind of application specific availability request.

In GRMG infrastructure we create a scenario with application and upload to GRMG, once we start the scenario it will ping the application with the specified time to check the application availability. It sends an http request to the application and expects an http request in response. If we get back the response infrastructure shows the application as available.

To support GRMG monitoring the developer has to develop the program to support GRMG.

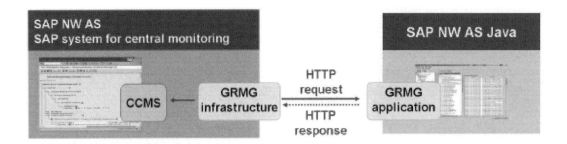

86   In our Java stacks lot of users are having authorizations issues with particular applications which are spread across our landscape, we would like to trace these users how can we do this?

In Java stack we have Single Activity Trace which can help trace particular users for their activities in the application.

All user actions that are processed within a called application are recorded. A separate Single Activity Trace is written on each component. The traces are combined using passports. Each request receives a passport, which is transferred to all of the components involved.

The SAT data is automatically written to a trace file for every request and component using the SAP Logging API. You can display this trace file using the Log Viewer.

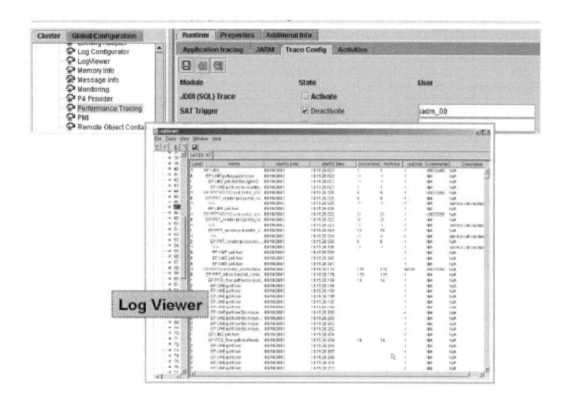

87   What is Global workload monitor in SAP Netweaver system? What are the common questions addressed by this tool?

The Global Workload Monitor displays the statistics data aggregated by the collector. You can use the functional trace (transaction STATTRACE), on the other hand, to display unaggregated raw statistics data for SAP ABAP systems and non-SAP-ABAP systems from complex system landscapes. The functional trace provides a finer granularity. With the functional trace, you can trace actions that belong to a single business process across system boundaries.

We can find answers to our common questions in the Global Workload Monitor:

- What is the workload of individual actions?
- How is the workload distributed across the individual hours of the day?
- Which action steps are showing the longest response and waiting times?
- What load data is collected when external components are called?
- What is the workload of individual users, and which actions have a user performed?

- What load is generated in a component due to actions of external components?

88 What is the new Maintenance Strategy SAP introduced with new business suites, can you explain?

SAP's maintenance strategy and support offerings have two dimensions: time and scope. In terms of the timeline, SAP defines three maintenance phases: mainstream maintenance, extended maintenance, and customer-specific maintenance. In terms of the scope, SAP offers three levels of support offerings: SAP Standard Support, SAP Premium Support, and SAP MaxAttention.

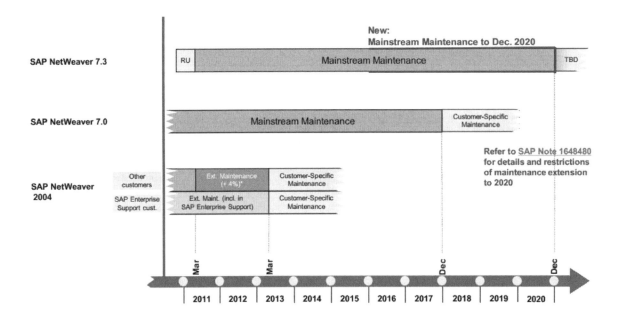

89   We have been listening from SAP ASAP methodology in past now we heard of new methodology called RunSAP what is this methodology is all about?

Run SAP methodology is recently adopeted by SAP for their operation maintainance of the customer landscape. ASAP methodology was dealing with all the product implementaions within in the customer landscape now we have RunSAP to better run the customer existing implemented solutions (End-to-End Solution Operations).

- The *SAP Standards for Solution Operations*
- The roadmap of *Run SAP* to implement *End-to-End Solution Operations*
- Training and certification program
- Tools, including the *SAP Solution Manager* application management platform
- Support services

The *Run SAP Roadmap* provides not only information on what needs to be implemented but also the how-to descriptions as*Implementation Methodology* and *Best Practices* documents.

The *Implementation Methodology* documents describe how the support scenarios are implemented across the life cycle *Design, Setup and Operations & Optimization*.

The *Best Practices* documents describe on more detail "how to implement" the End-to-End Solution Operations for different SAP business scenarios based on SAP's experience with thousands of customers.

90 **We have been Listening capabilities of SAP Netweaver are very broad, can you explain use the usage types and possibilities with SAP Netweaver?**

SAP systems are configured for a certain purpose, as indicated by usage types. The definition of usage types follows:

- Are structuring element for SAP software on a technical level.
- Determine the intended purpose of a system.
- Are realized by installing and configuring a collection of software components.
- May require other usage types in the same system to operate.

The following lists the usage types for SAP NetWeaver:

- Application Server ABAP (AS ABAP)
- Application Server Java (AS Java)
- Enterprise Portal Core (EPC)
- Enterprise Portal (EP)
- Business Intelligence (BI)
- Business Intelligence Java Components (BI Java)
- Development Infrastructure (DI)
- Mobile Infrastructure (MI)
- Process Integration (PI)

91	**We have our old SAP landscape planning to upgrade to new ERP solution provided by SAP, but we came to know we have to move to UNICODE system before we make our way to upgrade what is this Unicode is all about?**

According to standard definition of Unicode:

"Unicode is the encoding standard which provides the basis for processing, storage and interchange of text data in any language in all modern software and information technology protocols "
In Past SAP use to provide all language support for major languages to enable them working in their own native language … even we could have multiple languages supported in single installations called code pages. Unlike Unicode defines a character set that includes virtually all characters used worldwide and as a result provides consistent global character encoding.

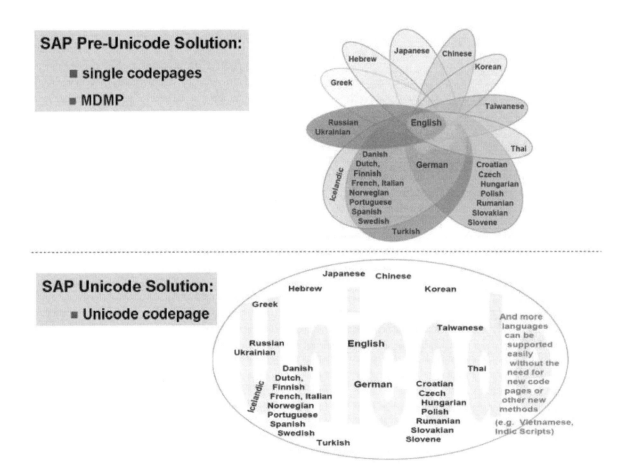

Up to and including SAP ERP 2004, SAP has provided multiple language support using single code pages as well as multiple code pages in a single installation with MDMP (Multi-Display-Multi-processing), which permits the application server to dynamically switch code pages according to the logon language and language keys (see SAP note 73606). However, even in an MDMP system, an individual user can use only the characters belonging to one code page at a time. To enhance language support for SAP Business Suite, SAP considers Unicode the appropriate development

direction and strategy because Unicode offers a single, consistent, and standard character set encoding for virtually all languages in the world. A code page describes the assignment of one character to one hexadecimal (HEX) value. One (normal: 1 byte) code page represents 256 characters.

92   How to install SAP License for a newly installed SAP system?

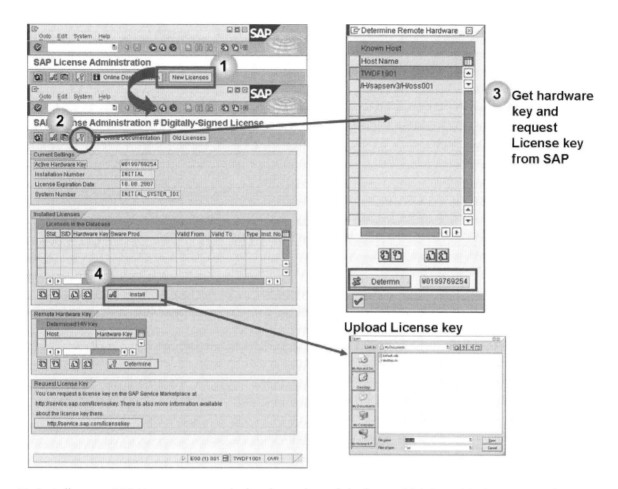

To install a new SAP License we need a hardware key of the host which host SAP instance and request a SAP license from SAP Service Marketplace, procedure goes as follows:

We can use transaction SLICENSE to determine the hardware key on all computers where an RFC connection is maintained.

On the initial screen of the transaction SLICENSE, choose *New Licenses*.

Now choose *Goto → Determine remote hardware key*. Select the *Hostname* and choose *Determine* to execute *saplicense* .

Get on the selected computer and to receive the hardware key as a result.

Use this hardware key to request a license at SAP.

You can install a new SAP License on your SAP system using the SLICENSE transaction.

Choose *Edit → Install License* and upload the license file you received from SAP. After the license is installed, the license key is activated immediately. After that, *Saplicense .install* is executed on the computer.

93   We have a newly installed system and we need to copy client for production usage. What will be the procedure to copy a client in SAP system?

As per the SAP recommendation production client must be a copy of the SAP reference client 000.

1. Maintain the new client with transaction SCC4

2. Activate kernel user SAP*

   • Set the profile parameter login/no_automatic_user_sapstar to 0

   • Restart the application server

3. Log on to the new client with kernel user SAP* and password PASS

4. Copy the client with transaction SCCL and profile SAP_CUST

5. Check the log files with transaction SCC3

6. Create the required users. These users must have at least the authorizations required for user administration and system administration. Create a user SAP* with all required authorizations for this user. If you want to have other users for system administration, you can also create user SAP* without authorizations.

7. Deactivate kernel user SAP*

   • Reset login/no_automatic_user_sapstar to 1

   • Restart the application server

94   When might we need to activate the extension set in a SAP ECC system?

For Activation of extension set we have 2 simple steps go to SPRO and choose -> activate SAP ECC Extension Set:

1. Call transaction SPRO (IMG).

2. Choose *SAP Reference IMG*.

From the technical point of view, SAP ERP Central Component Extensions are delivered and installed as part of an Add-On for SAP ERP Central Component, which is SAP ERP Central Component Extension Set. Client-independent activation switches allow us to use the functions contained in SAP ERP Central Component Extension Set components.

After activating, the Business Transaction Events (BTEs) and BAdI implementations marked as SAP-internal and already activated in a static way are also executed at runtime. After the activation, additional entries display in the tree structures of IMG, Application Component Hierarchy (ACH), and the default SAP Easy Access Menu based on the component activated.

Generally, we cannot deactivate an activated switch because data is updated in a different way than it would be if the relevant component was inactive. This depends on the component and the actions performed in the system after activation. Before we activate parts of SAP ERP Central Component, ensure that no clients are marked as **productive** in the system.

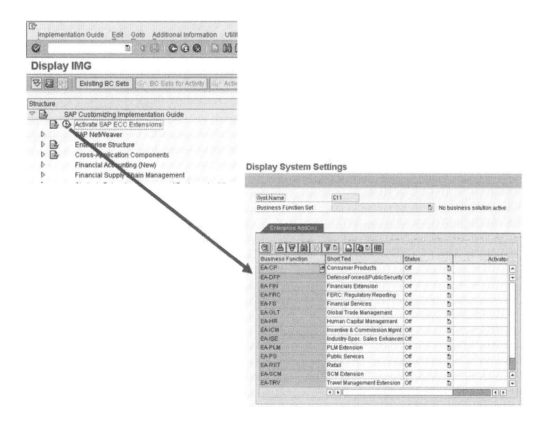

95   We are setting up our backup strategy for Java stack what are the bullet points to be considered. What should be the contents of our backup?

A complete backup of all changes to SAP NW AS Java since the installation consists of:

- Backing Up the Databases
- Backing up the file system: Global directory \usr\sap\<SID>

To ensure that no changes are made to the file system during the backup, the

SDM should be stopped

- Backing up the instance configuration (export by means of Configtool)

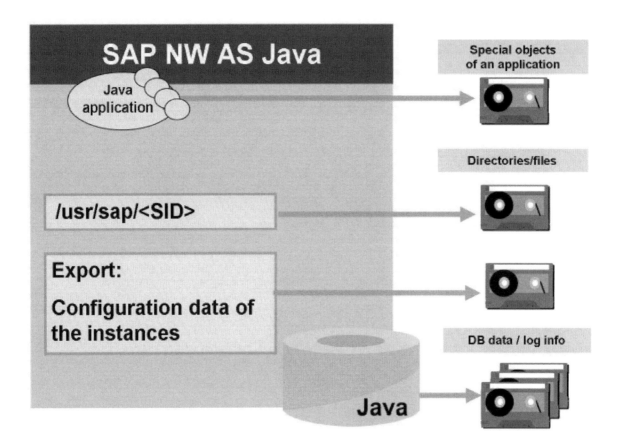

96   We are setting up printing strategy for our SAP Landscape, what is the concept of logical server in SAP spool system?

A **spool server** is an SAP application server with at least one spool work process. Every output request is processed on a real spool server of this type. An output device created in the SAP system can be assigned a spool server directly. However, there are many advantages associated with an additional logical layer between the output device and the spool server. We can use **logical (spool) servers** for this purpose. These stand for a hierarchy of other logical servers and/or real spool servers.

You can classify output devices and spool servers, for example, for test printing or production printing. The SAP system checks the classifications when saving, and displays a warning message if there are deviations. For example, the system warns us if you attempt to assign a high volume printer to a production print server.

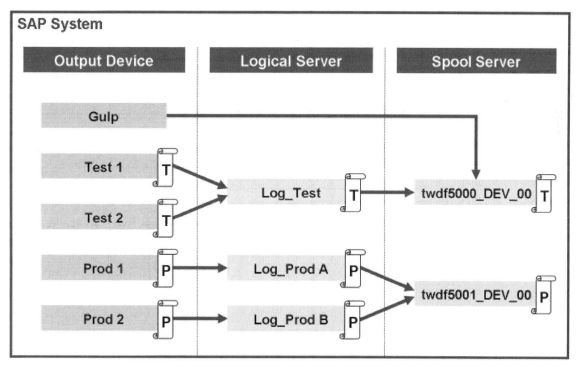

97   **What will be the backup strategy for printing server, we are having multiple print servers so we would like to have a backup print server for our main server?**

When creating a spool server (either a logical server or a spool server), we can specify an **alternative server**. If the normal server is not available, the SAP system attempts to use this alternative.

We must ensure that all printers that may be used by a different spool server can be controlled in the same way by every spool server.

You cannot define more than two spool servers for a logical server. Since a logical server can itself reference logical servers, **extensive spool server hierarchies** are also possible.

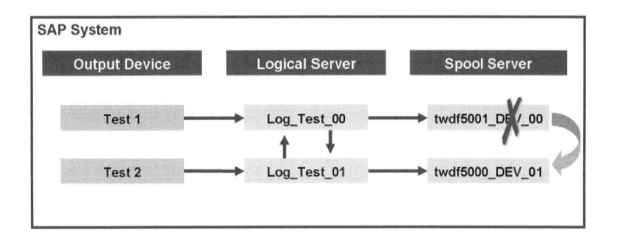

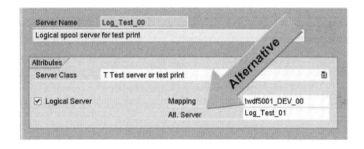

98   Within SAP Background job processing what are the possible statuses a background job can have? Can you explain in detail?

In SAP background a job can have the following statuses:

Scheduled

The steps that make up the job have already been defined; however the start condition still needs defining.

Released

The job has been completely defined, including its start condition. A job cannot be released without a start condition. Only an administrator or a user with the relevant authorizations for background processing can release a job. This ensures that unauthorized users cannot execute jobs without approval.

Ready

The start condition of a released job has been fulfilled. A job scheduler has placed the job in the wait queue for a free background work process.

Active

The job is currently being executed and cannot be deleted or changed. If an active job does not seem to be running correctly (for example, it is running for an unusually long time), you can terminate it in a background work process in debugging mode, analyse it, and then either release it again or terminate it completely. To do this, in transaction SM37, choose *Job → Capture: active job*.

Finished

All steps of this job were successfully completed.

Cancelled

The job aborted. This can happen in two ways:

- An administrator deliberately terminates the job in transaction SM37 by choosing *Job → Cancel active job*.

- A job step is terminated with an error.

99 In SAP system we have some standard jobs that we can schedule with in SAP system from where and how can we schedule them?

Standard jobs are background jobs that should run regularly in a production SAP system. These jobs mainly perform certain clean up tasks in the system, such as the deletion of obsolete spool requests. In the job definition transaction (SM36), we can access a selection of important standard jobs that we can schedule, monitor, and edit by choosing *Standard Jobs*.

- If we want to schedule all standard jobs, choose *Default Scheduling*. All standard jobs that are defined in table REORGJOBS are scheduled with the specified variant and period. If other jobs exist that execute one of the programs of the standard jobs, the system informs we of this.

- To schedule individual jobs, choose the selected job with the input help and specify an execution period.

- To define an additional standard job that is not yet available in the selection (table *REORGJOBS*), choose *Predefine new job*.

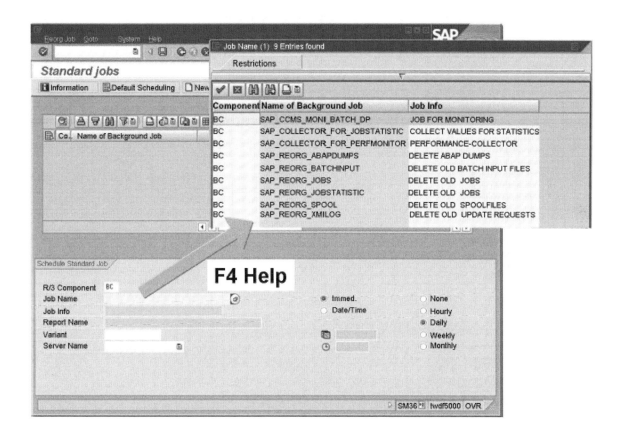

100   What are the possible events in an SAP system which we can use to trigger the SAP Background job?

An application server is specified for the processing of events that are triggered within the SAP system in profile parameter *rdisp/btcname*. An event-dependent job scheduler is started on this server. This scheduler checks whether a job is waiting for the event that has been received. It is therefore important that the parameter *rdisp/btcname* contains the name of an active background server.

Event-dependent jobs can be scheduled with one of the following three start conditions:

After event

The job starts after a defined event is received by the SAP system.

At operation mode

With this option, you can link a job to the activation of an operation mode when scheduling the job.

After job

In this way, you can create simple job chains where the execution of the successor job can be made dependent on the status of the predecessor job.

Made in the USA
San Bernardino, CA
12 March 2013